MW00768173

THE REAL THING

**Contemporary Documents
in American Government**

The St. Martin's Resource Library in Political Science

THE REAL THING

Contemporary Documents in American Government

Fengyan Shi
Georgetown University

St. Martin's Press
New York

Library of Congress Catalog Card Number: 96-70448

Manufactured in the United States of America.
1 0 9 8 7
f e d c b

For information, write:
St. Martin's Press
175 Fifth Avenue
New York, NY 10010

ISBN: 0-312-15355-4

PREFACE

The Real Thing: Contemporary Documents in American Government shows students some of the artifacts of today's government: bills, laws, Supreme Court opinions, presidential correspondence, and publications by executive agencies and interest groups. It is designed to supplement St. Martin's core texts in American Government and is organized parallel to them, starting with documents concerning the Constitution and ending with a set on the institutions. We have reproduced each document to look as it does in real life. By using high-quality photography or line art, *The Real Thing* gives students an opportunity to glimpse the government at work and to make relevant the abstract ideas presented in the study of American Government.

The Real Thing is part of the St. Martin's Resource Library in Political Science, a series of short books that supplement the study of political science. They are available free, or for a nominal price, to adopters of a St. Martin's core text.

Fengyan Shi

CONTENTS

The St. Martin's Resource Library in Political Science

THE REAL THING

**Contemporary Documents
in American Government**

1 The Proposed Balanced Budget Amendment

By a 300-to-132 vote, this proposed constitutional amendment requiring a balanced federal budget was passed by the House of Representatives on January 26, 1995. The roll-call vote margin in the Senate was one vote short of the required two-thirds majority (67 votes); however, the Senate majority leader at that time, Bob Dole, changed his vote to a "no" in order to reintroduce the measure later on the Senate legislative calendar. The final vote in the Senate was 65 to 35.

Calendar No. 18

104TH CONGRESS
1ST SESSION
H. J. RES. 1

IN THE SENATE OF THE UNITED STATES

JANUARY 27 (legislative day, JANUARY 10), 1995
Received; read twice and placed on the calendar

JOINT RESOLUTION

Proposing a balanced budget amendment to the Constitution of the United States.

1   *Resolved by the Senate and House of Representatives*
2   *of the United States of America in Congress assembled*
3   *(two-thirds of each House concurring therein),* That the fol-
4   lowing article is proposed as an amendment to the Con-
5   stitution of the United States, which shall be valid to all
6   intents and purposes as part of the Constitution when
7   ratified by the legislatures of three-fourths of the several
8   States within seven years after the date of its submission
9   to the States for ratification:

Document of the U.S. House of Representatives.

1   "ARTICLE —

2   "SECTION 1. Total outlays for any fiscal year shall

3 not exceed total receipts for that fiscal year, unless three-

4 fifths of the whole number of each House of Congress shall

5 provide by law for a specific excess of outlays over receipts

6 by a rollcall vote.

7   "SECTION 2. The limit on the debt of the United

8 States held by the public shall not be increased, unless

9 three-fifths of the whole number of each House shall pro-

10 vide by law for such an increase by a rollcall vote.

11   "SECTION 3. Prior to each fiscal year, the President

12 shall transmit to the Congress a proposed budget for the

13 United States Government for that fiscal year in which

14 total outlays do not exceed total receipts.

15   "SECTION 4. No bill to increase revenue shall become

16 law unless approved by a majority of the whole number

17 of each House by a rollcall vote.

18   "SECTION 5. The Congress may waive the provisions

19 of this article for any fiscal year in which a declaration

20 of war is in effect. The provisions of this article may be

21 waived for any fiscal year in which the United States is

22 engaged in military conflict which causes an imminent and

23 serious military threat to national security and is so de-

24 clared by a joint resolution, adopted by a majority of the

25 whole number of each House, which becomes law.

1   "SECTION 6. The Congress shall enforce and imple-

2 ment this article by appropriate legislation, which may rely

3 on estimates of outlays and receipts.

4   "SECTION 7. Total receipts shall include all receipts

5 of the United States Government except those derived

6 from borrowing. Total outlays shall include all outlays of

7 the United States Government except for those for repay-

8 ment of debt principal.

9   "SECTION 8. This article shall take effect beginning

10 with fiscal year 2002 or with the second fiscal year begin-

11 ning after its ratification, whichever is later.".

Passed the House of Representatives January 26, 1995.

Attest: ROBIN H. CARLE,

Clerk.

2 The Proposed Term Limit Amendment

This proposed constitutional amendment, as introduced in the U.S. House of Representatives, was designed to limit the terms of members of Congress. Despite broad support by the American public, the amendment failed to pass the House of Representatives by a roll-call vote of 227 to 204 on March 29, 1995. In the Senate, the effort to bring the amendment to a vote was blocked by a Democratic filibuster on April 23, 1996.

House Calendar No. 27

104TH CONGRESS
1ST SESSION

H. J. RES. 2

[Report No. 104–67]

Proposing an amendment to the Constitution of the United States with respect to the number of terms of office of Members of the Senate and the House of Representatives.

IN THE HOUSE OF REPRESENTATIVES

JANUARY 4, 1995

Mr. McCOLLUM, Mr. HANSEN, Mr. PETERSON of Minnesota, and Mr. LoBIONDO (for themselves, Mr. LIGHTFOOT, Mr. GILLMOR, Mr. ALLARD, Mr. ARMEY, Mr. BACHUS, Mr. BAKER of California, Mr. BALLENGER, Mr. BARCIA, Mr. BARR, Mr. BARRETT of Nebraska, Mr. BARTLETT of Maryland, Mr. BASS, Mr. BEREUTER, Mr. BILBRAY, Mr. BILIRAKIS, Mr. BLUTE, Mr. BONILLA, Mr. BROWNBACK, Mr. BRYANT, Mr. BUNNING of Kentucky, Mr. BURR, Mr. BUYER, Mr. CALVERT, Mr. CAMP, Mr. CANADY of Florida, Mr. CHAMBLISS, Mr. CHRISTENSEN, Mr. COBLE, Mr. COLLINS of Georgia, Mr. COOLEY, Mr. CRANE, Mr. CREMEANS, Mr. CUNNINGHAM, Mr. DEAL of Georgia, Mr. DIAZ-BALART, Mr. DICKEY, Mr. DOOLITTLE, Ms. DUNN of Washington, Mr. ENGLISH of Pennsylvania, Mr. ENSIGN, Mr. EVERETT, Mr. EWING, Mr. FIELDS of Texas, Mr. FLANAGAN, Mr. FOLEY, Mr. FORBES, Mr. FOX of Pennsylvania, Mr. FRANKS of Connecticut, Mr. FRISA, Mr. FUNDERBURK, Mr. GALLEGLY, Mr. GANSKE, Mr. GEKAS, Mr. GOODLATTE, Mr. GOSS, Mr. GRAHAM, Mr. GREENWOOD, Mr. GUNDERSON, Mr. GUTKNECHT, Mr. HANCOCK, Ms. HARMAN, Mr. HASTINGS of Washington, Mr. HAYWORTH, Mr. HILLEARY, Mr. HOBSON, Mr. HOEKSTRA, Mr. HOKE, Mr. HORN, Mr. HOUGHTON, Mr. HUTCHINSON, Mr. INGLIS of South Carolina, Mr. ISTOOK, Mr. SAM JOHNSON of Texas, Mr. KIM, Mr. KINGSTON, Mr. KLUG, Mr. KNOLLENBERG, Mr. LaHOOD, Mr. LATHAM, Mr. LaTOURETTE, Mr. LAZIO of New York, Mr. LEACH, Mr. LEWIS of Kentucky, Mr. LINDER, Mr. LUCAS, Mr. MANZULLO, Mr. MARTINI, Mr. McCRERY, Mr. McINTOSH, Mr. McKEON, Mr. MEEHAN, Mr. METCALF, Mr. MICA, Mr. MILLER of Florida, Mr. MINGE, Mrs. MYRICK, Mr. NEUMANN, Mr. NEY, Mr. NORWOOD, Mr. NUSSLE, Mr. PACKARD, Mr. PAXON, Mr. POMBO, Mr. PORTMAN, Ms. PRYCE, Mr. QUINN, Mr.

Document of the U.S. House of Representatives.

RAMSTAD, Mr. RADANOVICH, Mr. RIGGS, Mr. ROHRABACHER, Mr. ROYCE, Mr. SAXTON, Mr. SCARBOROUGH, Mr. SCHAEFER, Mrs. SEASTRAND, Mr. SHADEGG, Mr. SHAW, Mr. SMITH of Michigan, Mr. SMITH of Texas, Mr. SOLOMON, Mr. SOUDER, Mr. STEARNS, Mr. STOCKMAN, Mr. STUMP, Mr. TALENT, Mr. TAYLOR of North Carolina, Mr. THORNBERRY, Mr. TIAHRT, Mr. TORKILDSEN, Mr. UPTON, Mrs. WALDHOLTZ, Mr. WAMP, Mr. WELLER, Mr. WHITE, Mr. WHITFIELD, Mr. WILSON, Mr. ZELIFF, Mr. ZIMMER, and Mr. McINNIS) introduced the following joint resolution; which was referred to the Committee on the Judiciary

MARCH 6, 1995

Additional sponsors: Mr. HAYES, Mrs. MEYERS of Kansas, Mr. WALKER, Mr. DEUTSCH, Mr. COBURN, and Mr. GOODLING

Deleted sponsors: Mr. ALLARD (added January 4, 1995; deleted February 7, 1995), Mr. BROWNBACK (added January 4, 1995; deleted March 6, 1995), Mr. CHRISTENSEN (added January 4, 1995; deleted February 24, 1995), Mr. HILLEARY (added January 4, 1995; deleted March 1, 1995), Mr. KIM (added January 4, 1995; deleted February 22, 1995), Mr. McINTOSH (added January 4, 1995; deleted March 1, 1995), Mrs. MYRICK (added January 4, 1995; deleted March 6, 1995), Mr. ROYCE (added January 4, 1995; deleted March 1, 1995), Mrs. SEASTRAND (added January 4, 1995; deleted March 3, 1995), and Mr. TALENT (added January 4, 1995; deleted February 13, 1995)

MARCH 6, 1995

Reported with an amendment, referred to the House Calendar, and ordered to be printed

[Strike out all after the resolving clause and insert the part printed in italic]

JOINT RESOLUTION

Proposing an amendment to the Constitution of the United States with respect to the number of terms of office of Members of the Senate and the House of Representatives.

1   *Resolved by the Senate and House of Representatives*

2 *of the United States of America in Congress assembled*

3 *(two-thirds of each House concurring therein),* ~~That the fol-~~

4 ~~lowing article is proposed as an amendment to the Con-~~

1 stitution of the United States, which shall be valid to all

2 intents and purposes as part of the Constitution when

3 ratified by the legislatures of three-fourths of the several

4 States within seven years from the date of its submission

5 by the Congress:

6 "ARTICLE —

7 "No person who has been elected to the Senate two

8 times shall be eligible for election or appointment to the

9 Senate. No person who has been elected to the House of

10 Representatives six times shall be eligible for election to

11 the House of Representatives.".

12 *That the following article is proposed as an amendment to*

13 *the Constitution of the United States:*

14 "ARTICLE —

15 "SECTION 1. *No person who has been elected for a full*

16 *term to the Senate two consecutive times shall be eligible*

17 *for election or appointment to the Senate for a third con-*

18 *secutive term. No person who has been elected for a full term*

19 *to the House of Representatives six consecutive times shall*

20 *be eligible for election to the House of Representatives for*

21 *a seventh consecutive term.*

22 "SECTION 2. *Service as a Senator or Representative*

23 *for more than half of a term to which someone else was*

24 *originally elected shall be considered an election for the pur-*

25 *poses of section 1.*

4

1   "SECTION 3. *This article shall be inoperative unless*
2   *it shall have been ratified by the legislatures of three-fourths*
3   *of the several States within seven years from the date of*
4   *its submission to the States by the Congress.*

5   "SECTION 4. *No election or service occurring before this*
6   *article becomes operative shall be taken into account when*
7   *determining eligibility for election under this article.*

8   "SECTION 5. *No provision of any State statute or con-*
9   *stitution shall diminish or enhance, directly or indirectly,*
10   *the limits set by this article.".*

7

2 FEDERALISM

Created by Public Law 86–38 in 1959, the Advisory Commission on Intergovernmental Relations (ACIR) is an independent bipartisan agency that studies the federal government's relationship with state, local, and tribal governments. The Commission is composed of twenty-six members who are appointed by elected officials, including the president. Its mission is "to strengthen the American federal system and to improve the ability of federal, state, and local government to work together cooperatively, efficiently, and effectively." The following two documents reveal issues of current concern to the ACIR.

3   The Unfunded Mandates

The issue of unfunded mandates is one of the most controversial issues currently affecting the relationship between federal, state, and local governments. The Unfunded Mandates Reform Act of 1995 directed the ACIR "to investigate and review the role of federal mandates in intergovernmental relations" and to submit recommendations for reform to the president and Congress. In compliance with that statute, the ACIR issued its criteria for reviewing unfunded mandates in July 1995; by September, it had selected fourteen specific mandates for intensive review. On January 24, 1996, the Commission published its preliminary report on the issue for public review and comment. Presented here are excerpts from that report, *The Role of Federal Mandates in Intergovernmental Relations*. The final version of the report is scheduled to be published by the end of 1996.

Document of the Advisory Commission on Intergovernmental Relations.

COMMON ISSUES

ACIR's review of existing mandates found a number of common issues that are troubling federal, state, and local government relations. These issues and ACIR's proposed recommendations to address them include:

1. Detailed procedural requirements. State and local governments are not given flexibility to meet national goals in ways that best fit their needs and resources. The imposition of exact standards or detailed requirements, in many instances, merely increases costs and delays achievement of the national goals. *The federal role in implementation should be to provide research and technical advice for those governments that request it, but, in general, state and local governments should be permitted to comply with a mandate in a manner that best suits their particular needs and conditions.*

2. Lack of federal concern about mandate costs. When the federal government imposes costs on another government without providing federal funds, the magnitude of costs is often not considered. If the federal government has no financial obligation, it has little incentive to weigh costs against benefits or to allow state and local governments to determine the least costly alternatives for reaching national goals. *The federal government should assume some share of mandate costs as an incentive to restrain the extent of the mandate and to aid in seeking the least costly alternatives.*

3. Federal failure to recognize state and local governments' public accountability. State governments often are treated as just another interest group, as private entities, or as administrative arms of the federal government, not as sovereign governments with powers derived from the U.S. Constitution. Local governments, despite the important role they play in delivering government services, have been given even less consideration. Non-governmental advocacy groups' views have sometimes been given more attention than those of state and local governments. *Federal laws should recognize that state and local governments are led by elected officials who must account to the voters for their actions, just as the President and Members of Congress.*

4. Lawsuits by individuals against state and local governments to enforce federal mandates. Many federal laws permit individuals or organizations to sue state and local governments over questions of compliance, even though a federal agency is responsible for enforcement. Federal laws, however, are often written in such broad terms, it is not clear what is required of federal, state, and local officials. In these circumstances, permitting litigation brought by individuals subjects state and local governments to budgetary uncertainties and substantial legal costs. Because the federal agency is not directly involved with the costs and problems of this litigation, it has little incentive to propose amendments that would clarify the law's requirements. *Only the federal agency responsible for enforcement of a law should be permitted to sue state and local governments.*

5. Inability of very small local governments to meet mandate standards and timetables. The requirements for many federal mandates are based on the assumption that all local governments have the financial, administrative, and technical resources that exist in large governments. Many very small local governments have only part-time staffs with little technical capability and very limited resource bases. Extending deadlines or modifying requirements for these small governments may have minimal adverse effects on the achievement of overall national goals but may make it possible for such governments eventually to comply. *Deadlines should be extended and requirements modified for very small local governments.*

6. Lack of coordinated federal policy with no federal agency empowered to make binding decisions about a mandate's requirements. There are mandates that involve several federal agencies. This has resulted in confusion about what the law requires and how state and local governments can know when they are in compliance. In addition to making state and local governments aware of mandate requirements, federal agencies should explain the reasons for the mandate and should assist in taking the actions necessary for implementation. *A single federal agency should be designated to coordinate each mandate's implementation and to make binding decisions about that mandate.*

SUMMARY OF RECOMMENDATIONS ON INDIVIDUAL MANDATES

ACIR's proposed recommendations for individual mandates can be summarized into three categories.

The Commission finds that the following mandates as they apply to state and local governments do *not* have a sufficient national interest to justify intruding on state and local government abilities to control their own affairs. While the Commission does not take issue with the goals of these mandates, it believes that achieving those goals can be left to elected state and local officials. **Thus, ACIR recommends repealing the provisions in these laws that extend coverage to state and local governments.**

>*Fair Labor Standards Act*
>
>*Family and Medical Leave Act*
>
>*Occupational Safety and Health Act*
>
>Drug and Alcohol Testing of Commercial Drivers

5

Metric Conversion for Plans and Specifications

Medicaid: Boren Amendment

Required Use of Recycled Crumb Rubber

The Commission finds that the following mandates are necessary because national policy goals justify their use. However, the federal share of the costs should be increased or the stringent requirements and deadlines imposed on state and local governments should be relaxed. These mandates impose substantial costs on state and local governments as a result of requirements that are unnecessarily burdensome. **Thus, ACIR recommends retaining these mandates with modifications to accommodate budgetary and administrative constraints on state and local governments.**

The Clean Water Act

Individuals with Disabilities Education Act

Americans with Disabilities Act

The Commission finds the following mandates are related to acceptable national policy goals, but they should be revised to provide greater flexibility in implementation procedures and more participation by state and local governments in development of mandate policies. **Thus, ACIR recommends revising these mandates to provide greater flexibility and increased consultation.**

The Safe Drinking Water Act

Endangered Species Act

The Clean Air Act

Davis-Bacon Related Acts

4   The Family and Medical Leave Act

In the ACIR's preliminary report on unfunded mandates, the fourteen mandates selected for review were categorized into three groups: those to be repealed, those to be modified, and those to be revised. The Family and Medical Leave Act of 1993 (FMLA) is an example in the first category—one of those to be repealed. The following brief review of FMLA by the ACIR staff appears in the report mentioned previously.

Staff Working Paper
December 1, 1995

FAMILY AND MEDICAL LEAVE ACT

Mandate

The *Family and Medical Leave Act of 1993* (FMLA) (29 U.S.C., 2601 et seq.) requires employers to provide employees up to 12 weeks of unpaid leave each year to care for a newborn, adopted, or foster child. Leave also must be granted for care of a seriously ill child, parent, or spouse. In addition, employees may use unpaid family and medical leave for personal illnesses. Medical insurance benefits must be continued during the leave and employees must be reinstated into the same or an equivalent position after leave.

Background

FMLA was enacted to promote family stability and economic security among working men and women. At the time of enactment, the General Accounting Office (GAO) calculated that the primary costs associated with FMLA would relate to extending medical benefits and hiring and training temporary replacement workers, or other measures taken to maintain an employee's production output during the unpaid leave period. Some cost avoidance was anticipated for employers based on reduced employee turnover rates, anticipated higher productivity, and reduced need for hiring and training permanent replacement workers. It was thought that the cost of implementation would be mitigated by the fact that many employers, including 11 states and the District of Columbia, followed similar practices.

Concerns

State and local governments raise several concerns with the FLSA. First, they argue that the law sometimes contradicts state or local government leave provisions. In fact, rather than exempting jurisdictions that had family and medical leave policies, the federal law preempted those policies, except in the case of more generous benefits. Also, some claim that FMLA compromises collective bargaining negotiations between state and local governments and public employee unions.

A second issue is the inflexibility of the Department of Labor's interpretation of the law. Rather than allowing variable family and medical leave policies that are consistent with FMLA, state and local governments have been required to match the department's regulations. For example, even though the law does not specify the length of time an employee must return to work to avoid repayment of medical premiums, states are required to abide by the federal regulatory provision that sets the return-to-work period at 30 days. So, if an employee is absent for the allowable 12 weeks, a state may pay 3 months worth of medical premiums and the employee is only required to return to

A-5

Document of the Advisory Commission on Intergovernmental Relations.

work for 30 days to avoid having to reimburse any portion. Some states have suggested that employees be required to return to work for at least as long as they were absent or 30 days, whichever is greater, to avoid reimbursement charges. Such a policy could be considered consistent with the law but is not allowed under federal regulations.

Finally, FMLA is seen by state and local governments as an unfunded federal mandate because of the cost associated with the extension of medical insurance benefits and other factors. As noted above, these costs were anticipated by GAO prior to the law's enactment. Unanticipated, however, were the reportedly significant costs related to training personnel specialists on the law's provisions and the time spent counseling individual employees. In addition, record-keeping requirements related to tracking of FMLA leave have added costs, especially in cases where both spouses work for the same employer.

Recommendation Options

1. Make no significant changes in the law. FMLA grants a significant benefit to employees struggling to balance family and work responsibilities. The act makes a positive contribution toward the national policy objective of strengthening family stability and improving economic security for working men and women. Thus, it could be argued that the benefits to the nation are worth the costs and that it is the rightful responsibility of employers—public and private—to fund the act's implementation. Nevertheless, some changes in the law could be made to allow for closer conformity between the federal law and state or local policies.

2. Exempt state and local governments from FMLA provisions. The family and medical leave policies of state or local governments would be a matter of concern solely within the respective jurisdictions. This would recognize the public accountability aspects of state and local governments, and it would acknowledge the authority of these governments to conduct collective bargaining with public employee unions unhindered by federal preconditions.

3. Give state governments independent regulatory and enforcement responsibility for compliance with the law in the public sector. State governments would be granted the same authority as the federal government to set their own family and medical leave policies consistent with FMLA. Currently, the law allows the Office of Personnel Management rather than the Department of Labor to issue regulations and enforce FMLA policies for the executive branch. Likewise, there are special provisions for congressional employees. Such an approach would not exempt a state from complying with the law, but would allow it flexibility to set its own policies consistent with the law. If challenged by an employee, the state would be responsible for the defense of its own policies and not those of the federal government.

A-6

13

3 CIVIL RIGHTS AND LIBERTIES

5 The Due Process of Law

The Fifth and Fourteenth Amendments provide that no person shall "be deprived of life, liberty, or property without due process of law." "Due process of law" refers to those legal proceedings that have been established for the protection of individual rights. The flowcharts presented here illustrate the typical progression of actions in a civil or criminal proceeding in a federal district court. These charts are from *Understanding the Federal Courts*, published by the Administrative Office of the United States Courts, which is responsible for administering the entire U.S. federal court system. *Understanding the Federal Courts* (1995) provides an overview of the basic structure and functions of this system.

**Trial Progression
of Civil Actions**

Complaint Filed

Answer Filed

Discovery Proceedings

Motions Filed Relating
to Discovery Matters

Pretrial Proceedings

Trial by Judge
or Jury

Termination by Judge
or Jury Verdict

Courtesy of the Administrative Office of the United States Courts.

Trial Progression
of Criminal Actions

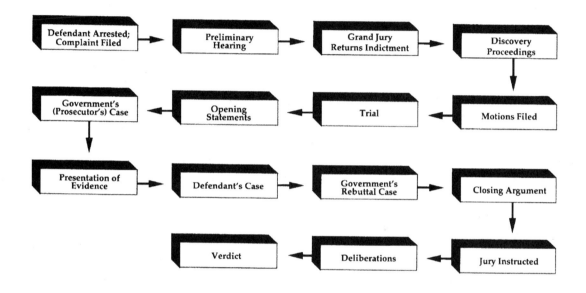

6 A Miranda Rights Card

In the United States, when a police officer arrests someone, the officer must "read their rights" to the arrested individual(s) on the spot. The card from which the police officer reads is called the Miranda Rights Card. In the Miranda decision, the Supreme Court held that as soon as an arrest is made, arrested persons must be told of their right to remain silent and their right to have a lawyer, who will be provided if they cannot afford one. Printed here is a Miranda Rights Card currently in use by the police department of Phoenix, Arizona, where *Miranda v. Arizona* (1966) was tried. The front side of the card is in English; the opposite side is in Spanish.

PPD #29   Rev. 11/87

YOU HAVE THE RIGHT TO REMAIN SILENT

ANYTHING YOU SAY CAN BE USED AGAINST YOU IN A COURT OF LAW

YOU HAVE THE RIGHT TO THE PRESENCE OF AN ATTORNEY TO ASSIST YOU PRIOR TO QUESTIONING, AND TO BE WITH YOU DURING QUESTIONING, IF YOU SO DESIRE.

IF YOU CANNOT AFFORD AN ATTORNEY YOU HAVE THE RIGHT TO HAVE AN ATTORNEY APPOINTED FOR YOU PRIOR TO QUESTIONING.

DO YOU UNDERSTAND THESE RIGHTS?

DATE   DR#   OFF INITIALS

Ud. tiene el derecho de guardar silencio.

Cualquier cosa que diga se puede usar en su contra en los tribunales de justicia.

Ud. tiene el derecho a que este presente un abogado para ayudarle antes del interrogatorio y que le acompane durante el interrogatorio, si Ud. lo desea.

Si Ud. no tiene los fondos para pagar a un abogado, tiene el derecho a que el tribunal nombre a uno para representarle antes de que se le interrogue.

Entiende Ud. estos derechos?

Courtesy of the Phoenix Police Department.

7   An Official Jury Summons

In *Duncan v. Louisiana* (1968), the U.S. Supreme Court held: "Trial by jury in criminal cases is fundamental to the American scheme of justice." A trial by a jury of the accused's peers is a practice that allows the power of the courts to be checked by the public. Here is a copy of a formal notice letter from the D.C. Superior Court (the trial court of the District of Columbia) to a potential jury candidate. Those who receive these letters form a jury pool from which a panel of jurors will be selected for specific cases.

OFFICE OF THE
CLERK OF THE SUPERIOR COURT
OF THE DISTRICT OF COLUMBIA
WASHINGTON, D.C. 20001-2131

PRESORTED
FIRST CLASS MAIL
U.S. POSTAGE
PAID
WASHINGTON, D.C.
PERMIT NO. 1726

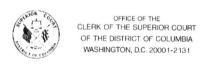

JURY SERVICE: IT'S FOR YOU
YOUR COURTS • YOUR COMMUNITY • YOUR RESPONSIBILITY

OFFICIAL JURY SUMMONS

TO:

Courtesy of the Superior Court of the District of Columbia.

DATE AND TIME TO REPORT	TYPE OF JUROR
WHERE TO REPORT	LENGTH OF SERVICE

SUPERIOR COURT OF THE DISTRICT OF COLUMBIA

SUMMONS FOR JURY SERVICE

BY ORDER OF THE CHIEF JUDGE OF THE SUPERIOR COURT OF THE DISTRICT OF COLUMBIA, YOU ARE HEREBY SUMMONED TO SERVE AS A JUROR AS INDICATED ABOVE. PLEASE COMPLETE THE ENCLOSED JUROR QUALIFICATION FORM AND RETURN IT WITHIN FIVE (5) DAYS. FAILURE TO APPEAR AS DIRECTED BY THIS SUMMONS MAY RESULT IN A FINE OF NOT MORE THAN THREE HUNDRED DOLLARS ($300) OR IMPRISONMENT FOR NOT MORE THAN SEVEN (7) DAYS OR BOTH. D.C. CODE 11-1907

PLEASE READ IMPORTANT INFORMATION ON THE BACK OF THIS FORM.

**DO NOT MAIL THIS FORM BACK.
BRING THIS SUMMONS WITH YOU.**

Clerk of the Court
Chief Judge

JUROR QUALIFICATION FORM — PLEASE READ AND PRINT YOUR ANSWERS TO THE QUESTIONS BELOW.

You are required by law to return this form, duly completed and signed, within five (5) days of its receipt. A prepaid envelope is enclosed for this purpose.

1. Are you a citizen of the United States? YES □ –1– NO □
2. Are you now and for all of the past six months have you been a resident of the District of Columbia? □ –2– □
3. Are you 18 years of age or older? □ –3– □
4. Can you read, speak and understand the English language? □ –4– □
5a. Are you hearing impaired? □ –5a– □
5b. If yes, are you requesting a sign-language interpreter? □ –5b– □
5c. Do you have any physical or mental disability which would not permit you to serve as a juror? If yes, explain briefly and enclose verifiable medical certificate. □ –5c– □
6. Have you come to court to serve on jury duty in the Superior Court of the District of Columbia within the last two years? If yes, give dates: □ –6– □
7. Do you have a pending felony or misdemeanor charge in any D.C, Federal or State Court? □ –7– □
8a. Have you ever been convicted of a felony? □ –8a– □
8b. If your answer to 8a was yes, has it been ten (10) years since the completion of your jail/prison term or parole, or probation? □ –8b– □
9a. If you work for a private employer, during your juror service will you receive your FULL salary? □ –9a– □
9b. If your answer to 9a was yes, does your employer require you to turn over your jury fee check to the company? □ –9b– □
10. Would you like to donate your $2.00 transportation fee to the court? □ –10– □

Juror's Social Security Number _____ Juror's Name _____

Home Tel. No.: _____ Business No.: _____ Age: _____ Sex: M □ F □

Ethnic Background: To assist in ensuring that all people are represented on juries, please indicate which of the following applies to you. Nothing disclosed will affect your selection for jury duty (see "Note" under IMPORTANT INFORMATION).
□ Black   □ White   □ Asian   □ Hispanic   □ American Indian
□ Other (specify) _____

Marital Status (check one): Single □ Married □ Divorced □ Separated □ Widow/Widower □

Highest level of education completed: _____

Address Change (if any) _____ Apt. _____ City _____ State _____ Zip _____

Employment (check one): Fed, D.C. State or Local Govt. □ Non-government □ Unemployed □ Retired □

Occupation (if retired, please list previous occupation): _____ Employer: _____

Employer's Address: _____

City _____ State _____ Zip Code _____

Any person who willfully misrepresents a material fact on a juror qualification form for the purpose of avoiding or receiving service as a juror may be fined not more than $300 or imprisoned not more than 90 days, or both. D.C. CODE 11-1906

RETURN THIS FORM WITHIN FIVE (5) DAYS — USE ENCLOSED ENVELOPE

I hereby certify under the penalties of perjury that any responses to the aforegoing questions are true to the best of my knowledge.

Date _____ Signature _____

Dear Citizen:

You have been randomly selected for jury service in the Superior Court of the District of Columbia. **The law requires that you complete and return the enclosed juror qualification form in the next five (5) days.** For general information regarding jury service, call **879-1604**.

LENGTH OF SERVICE

Your service as a juror will be either as a **trial juror** or a **grand juror**, as indicated on your summons. As a trial juror if you are selected to sit on a trial on the day you are summoned, you must be prepared to serve for the full length of the trial. **Since most trials last for several days, you must set your schedule accordingly.** If you are not selected for a trial on the day you are summoned, your service to the court will end, **unless you are required by the Clerk of the Court to return on the following day to continue the process, based on critical needs of the court.** Grand jurors serve no more than **25 work days** plus 2 "recall" days unless extended by the Chief Judge.

EXPENSE MONEY

Jurors who serve **only** one day are paid a $2.00 transportation allowance. Jurors who serve more than one day will be paid $2.00 per day for transportation plus a $30.00 jury fee for all days of service including the first day **except** that jurors who are full-time government employees (federal, state and local) and private sector employees **who are paid their normal salary** while on jury duty, will not receive a fee but will receive the $2.00 transportation allowance

EXCUSALS/DEFERRALS

District of Columbia law does not allow you to be excused from jury service based on the type of job you may hold. Your employer is required to give you time off from work to serve as a juror. If, however, there is a grave illness in your family or other serious problem which creates undue hardship or extreme inconvenience making it impossible for you to comply with the terms of this summons on the date(s) specified, please notify the Juror's Office immediately.

If you wish, you may receive one—**but only one**—deferral of your jury service. If you receive a deferral, **you must provide the Juror's Office with a mutually agreeable date on which you can serve. That date must be no later than 90 days after your original date. You must serve on the mutually agreed upon date. The deferred date must be one on which you will be available for several days in case you are selected for a trial.** The request for a deferral can be accomplished by calling 879-4604 **between the hours of 11:00 a.m. and 4:00 p.m.** within five (5) days of your receipt of this summons. You will not receive another summons for the deferred date. You must bring this original summons when you report for jury duty.

JURY SERVICE-DEMOCRACY IN ACTION

Jury service is one of the highest duties of citizenship. It also is an interesting experience that will teach you more about your system of justice and how it works. While jury service may require you to adjust your normal schedule, we hope that any inconvenience will be minimal and that you will enjoy the opportunity to participate in this vital process of our democratic society.

Sincerely,

Duane B. Delaney
Clerk of the Court

IMPORTANT INFORMATION

Selection Process:

Random selection from Voter Registration and Motor Vehicle Department rolls.

Warning:

Please be advised that dangerous items including weapons such as **"scissors", "pocket knives" or "swiss army knives"** are not allowed in the courthouse. Such dangerous items will be confiscated and they will **not** be returned due to a shortage of facilities to store such items. We also ask that you not bring **recording equipment, tape recorders or cameras** to the courthouse.

Non-Smoking Policy:

The Superior Court has been designated a "Smoke-Free" building. Smoking will **not be allowed** anywhere within any court buildings.

Employment Notice:

If you are a full-time government employee and serving on your day off, the court will need written verification that it is your day off so that you may be paid for your jury service if selected for a trial.

Attire:

Appropriate courtroom dress is required. Sweatsuits, work uniforms, and shorts are **not** acceptable. However, dress shorts of acceptable length (to be determined by the Juror Officer) will be allowed. Shirts, ties, dresses, suits, blazers, jackets and other business attire are appropriate. Improper dress will cause jurors to be sent home to change.

Note:

Ethnic Background: You are required as a prospective juror to indicate your ethnic background. This answer is required solely to avoid discrimination in juror selection and has absolutely no bearing on qualifications for jury service. By answering this question you help the court check and observe the juror selection process so that discrimination cannot occur. In this way the court can fulfill the policy of the United States which is to provide jurors who are randomly selected from a fair cross section of the community.

Available Services:

Child Care — A Child Care Center is located in Room 1225, at 500 Indiana Ave., N.W. Level One, to provide day care for children 24 months (must be toilet trained) to 14 years. This Center is open from 8:30 a.m. to 5:00 p.m. only, Monday through Friday. As the Center is unable to provide lunches, parents must either prepare a sack lunch or make arrangements to take the child out for lunch.

Health Unit — A Health Unit is located in Room 1195 at the Indiana Avenue entrance of the Courthouse. A staff of Registered Nurses is on duty Monday through Friday, 8:30 a.m. to 5:00 p.m.

Parking — Parking is not provided. Meter parking is discouraged since jurors will not have time available to keep their meters running. Public transportation is suggested.

8 A Juror Brochure

In 1995, the Superior Court Juror's Office of the District of Columbia summoned nearly 240,000 residents for jury service. There are two kinds of juries in the U.S. trial court system: the grand jury and the petit jury (or trial jury). Presented here is a brochure for petit jurors, which furnishes comprehensive information on jury service. One of the sections discusses the juror fee: In Washington, D.C., a juror is paid $2.00 per day, which is designated for transportation. Since the minimum Metrobus (or Metrorail) one-way fare has been raised to $1.10, the Court is considering raising the juror service fee to reimburse jurors' minimum transportation needs.

WELCOME

TO THE

SUPERIOR COURT

OF THE

DISTRICT OF COLUMBIA

Congratulations! You have been selected to perform an important role of citizenship that protects one of our country's most fundamental rights—TRIAL BY JURY. As a juror, you will be participating in a time-honored process that rests at the very heart of the American system of justice. You will be making decisions that affect the life, liberty or property rights of other citizens involved in cases before the court. Your responsibility will be to make a decision, along with your peers, based upon the law and the facts of a case without being influenced by sentiment, emotion, or bias.

This brochure provides basic information about your jury service. The Superior Court would like to take this opportunity to thank you in advance for your participation as a juror and for the invaluable role you are about to play in protecting our liberties and our system of justice.

DIAGRAM OF A COURTROOM

The following diagram represents the floor plan of a typical courtroom arrangement.

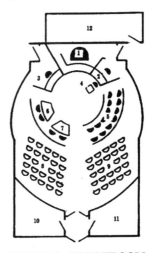

TYPICAL COURTROOM

1. JUDGE'S BENCH
2. WITNESS STAND
3. COURTROOM CLERK
4. COURT REPORTER
5. JURY BOX
6. DEFENDANT/ATTORNEY
7. PLAINTIFF/ATTORNEY
8. PUBLIC SEATING
9. PUBLIC SEATING
10. DEFENDANT WITNESS WAITING ROOM
11. PLAINTFF WITNESS WAITING ROOM
12. JURY DELIBERATION ROOM

4-0734 wd-327

Courtesy of the Superior Court of the District of Columbia.

THE SUPERIOR COURT
OF THE
DISTRICT OF COLUMBIA

The Superior Court of the District of Columbia is the trial court of general jurisdiction for the District of Columbia. The judiciary is comprised of 59 judges and 15 commissoners who are supported by over 1,000 administrative and support staff. The court is divided into six major divisions consisting of Civil, Criminal, Family, Probate, Multi-Door and Special Operations. The Criminal Division is responsible for felony, misdemeanor and traffic cases. The Civil Division hears all civil disputes including small claims, landlord and tenant matters. The Family Division handles divorces, adoptions, paternity, child support, mental health, mental retardation, child abuse, neglect, juvenile cases and marriages. The Probate Division is responsible for estates, guardianships, and conservatorships. The Multi-Door Division offers citizens the opportunity to resolve disputes through mediators and arbitrators without a trial in a neutral forum. The Special Operations Division is responsible for tax cases, appeals coordination, jury operations, interpreter services, child services and the law library.

The Executive Office and the Clerk of the Court's Office are responsible for the administration of all Superior Court operations under the direction of the Chief Judge.

TYPES OF JURY CASES

Juries decide two kinds of cases—civil cases and criminal cases.

A civil case is a dispute between two or more persons, or between the government and a person. It usually involves a claim for money damages, but may also involve the enforcement of a right or the resolution of any dispute not involving a criminal statute. Most civil cases involve claims for money damages and the jury's function is to determine the existence and extent of liability—not guilt or innocence.

A criminal case involves charging a person accused of committing an act against the public or society as a whole, with an offense in the name of the United States of America or the District of Columbia. The person charged is called the defendant. A criminal case begins with the filing of an information, which is a document filed by the government's attorney charging a person with committing an offense, or an indictment, which is a written accusation presented by a grand jury charging a person with an offense. When a defendant pleads not guilty to a charge, the case goes to trial. In a criminal case, the jury's responsibility is to decide if the defendant is guilty or not guilty of the charge stated in the "information or indictment".

JURY SERVICE
ONE TRIAL / ONE DAY

The Superior Court of the District of Columbia has a **ONE TRIAL/ONE DAY** term of jury service. This system represents the court's effort to reduce citizen inconvenience by effectively managing your time spent at the courthouse and ensuring that jurors are available for trials when the trial is ready to go forward. If you are not chosen to sit on a jury, you may only be at the courthouse for one day. However, on rare occassions, due to trial demand, you may be required by the Clerk of the Court to return the next day. Also it must be remembered that jury service is for one **entire trial OR one day.**

If you are selected to be a juror on a trial during your one day here, you must serve for the **entire** time it takes to complete that trial. Most trials last several days and, if selected, you must be prepared to serve no matter how long it takes. The court will not allow you to be excused because it is inconvenient for you to serve on a trial. You should plan to make the necessary arrangements with your employer and childcare providers and adjustments to your personal schedule so that you can serve longer than one day if required.

However, if you are not selected to serve as a juror on a trial during your one day of service you will be excused by the Juror Officer at approximately 5:00 p.m., depending on the court's needs. If you are selected to serve as a juror on a trial, you will be excused by the judge after the trial is completed. If this occurs, the judge will make every effort to release you as early as possible. When your One Day/One Trial juror service is complete, you will not be required to serve again for at least two years.

SELECTION OF JURORS

Your name was selected at random from a master file of District residents compiled from a list of registered voters, licensed drivers and non-drivers 18 years or older who have been issued identification cards.

If you have been charged with a crime or convicted of a crime that could result in imprisonment for more than one year, you cannot "qualify" as a juror until your civil rights have been restored, or at least ten years have passed since the completion of your entire sentence, including incarceration, probation, or parole. (Restoration of civil rights does not necessarily occur merely through the successful completion of a criminal sentence.) If you have any questions concerning your qualifications as a juror, please ask the Juror Officer or a member of the Juror's Office staff immediately.

PAYMENT OF JURORS

You will receive $2.00 per day as a travel allowance. If you are selected to serve on a trial you will receive an additional $30.00 per day, unless you are an employee of a Federal, State or Local Government Agency or of a private employer who pays your normal salary during your jury service. The law states that jurors who receive their normal salary from their employer can only be paid the $2.00 travel allowance for each day of service except in extenuating circumstances.

Jurors receive payment daily. You may obtain payment for your service at the Juror's Office on the afternoon of each day that you serve. If you do not obtain your payment by the end of the day, your payment for that day will be mailed to you.

Please be reminded that if the trial in which you are serving is recessed for an entire day for any reason, you are to report to work on that day. You will not be paid by the court for days on which a trial is in recess.

JUROR EMERGENCIES

If you have been assigned to a specific trial and become seriously ill or are involved in an emergency during non-work hours, call the Juror's Office at **879-4604** after 8:30 a.m. on the morning you cannot appear. Give the following information to the juror clerk that answers the telephone: state your name, clearly, the number of the courtroom to which you are assigned, the name of the judge in the case, and a telephone number where you can be reached if necessary. The Juror's Office will help you contact the presiding judge who may officially excuse you of good cause is shown.

JUROR ORIENTATION

If jury service is a new experience for you, you may be concerned that you will not know what to do. RELAX. The court and the Juror's Office will insure you receive all necessary information to prepare you to fulfill your role as a Juror.

Following your arrival and check-in, you will receive an orientation that will answer most of your concerns and explain your responsibilities as a Juror. As part of this orientation you will review a video that will provide you with the legal aspects of jury service and court proceedings. If you are assigned to a trial, the presiding judge will give you further instructions on proceedings and legal matters. The judge will decide if you may take notes in the courtroom and will explain other rules of the court, such as the fact that reading is not allowed in the courtroom.

JUROR PRIVACY

Juror's have the right to privacy regarding their telephone number and other personal information. Traditionally the court will not reveal the telephone number of a juror to other parties in the courtroom without the specific approval of the presiding judge. However, after a verdict has been reached, it is possible that the attorneys may wish to contact the jury so that they can ask opinions on a variety of topics such as assessment of their performance or the basis for the verdict. As a juror, you may respond if you wish, but **but you are under no obligation to do so** and may elect to remain silent. However, if you feel that you are being harassed or contacted for an inappropriate purpose, you should report the name of the attorney or party to the Juror's Office immediately.

WAITING IN THE LOUNGE

Please be prepared to spend time waiting in the Juror's Lounge prior to serving as a juror. We apologize for this inconvenience, but please know we are aware of your discontent. Many administrative processes have been implemented to minimize your waiting time and insure you are given the opportunity to serve as a juror. The waiting is caused by the fact that trials are scheduled to begin at different times throughout the day and parties may plead guilty in a criminal case or settle a civil case at any time prior to commencing the trial. Therefore, predicting when, or if, you will actually serve is very difficult.

Please be patient. The fact that available jurors are present in the courthouse and are ready to serve in trial and render a verdict may encourage parties to enter a guilty plea or resolve a dispute. Therefore, your mere presence in the courthouse actually serves the ends of justice.

During the day if the Juror's Office determines that you will not be needed because scheduled cases are resolved, every effort will be made to excuse you as early as possible. Our goal is not to inconvenience you any more than absolutely necessary. However, it is possible that after waiting all day you could be called to serve on a trial panel even after 4:00 p.m., and the panel could be held over until the next day if jury selection is not completed by the end of the day.

JUROR CONVENIENCE

In order to make you more comfortable while you are waiting to serve as a juror, the court provides the following basic conveniences:

1. Restrooms are located to the left when exiting the Juror's Lounge.

2. Pay telephones are available just inside the Juror's Lounge. A pay TDD telephone is also located in the lounge.

3. A child care center is available on the first floor for the use of jurors who have children who are potty trained and at least two years old.

4. A cafeteria is located on the lower level of the Courthouse (C Street Level). Vending machines are located in a room to the right when exiting the Juror's Lounge. (If you are not on a trial you will be excused for lunch from the Juror's Lounge by the Juror's Office. If you are on a trial, the judge will excuse you for lunch.)

5. Smoking is allowed only outside the Courthouse. The Courthouse is a "Smoke-Free" building and smoking is not allowed in any part of the Building.

6. A quiet room for jurors is located to the left when exiting the Juror's Lounge. You may wish to use this room for quiet activities such as reading or writing.

7. Lockers are located at the front of the Juror's Lounge and may be rented daily.

8. Medical attention may be requested through the Juror's Office or by notification of the judge. A nurse's office is located in Room 1195 on the first floor.

9. If someone needs to reach you in an emergency situation you may be contacted through the Juror's Office at 879-4604. The Juror Office will make every possible attempt to locate you.

9   An EEOC Report on Affirmative Action

The U.S. Equal Employment Opportunity Commission (EEOC) was created by Title VII of the Civil Rights Act of 1964, which was intended to eliminate discrimination based on race, color, religion, sex, or national origin. Since its establishment, the EEOC's jurisdictional mandate has been broadened by various legislative statutes and executive decrees. Among other things, the Commission publishes and distributes information to the general public regarding U.S. equal employment opportunity policies. The leaflet here was published by the EEOC in March 1996. It discusses the current status of affirmative action in employment from the EEOC's perspectives.

The EEOC and Affirmative Action in Employment

- The EEOC's statutory mandate is to enforce the federal laws that ensure equal employment opportunity for all, without regard to race, religion, ethnicity, gender, age or disability. The goal of these laws is to ensure that all Americans are judged on their ability to do the job, rather than on personal characteristics that have nothing to do with job performance.

- The laws enforced by the EEOC are based upon the promise of the 14th amendment to the Constitution that all Americans have a right to "equal protection" under the law.
  By enacting Title VII of the Civil Rights Act of 1964, Congress acknowledged that historic, systemic discrimination has created barriers for certain Americans to fulfillment of the promise of equal employment opportunity and a "level playing field." Accordingly, the Supreme Court has determined that, in **limited** circumstances, affirmative action is permitted under the Constitution and laws of the United States to help implement the civil rights laws and achieve equal opportunity for all.

- It is important to clarify that the extent of permissible affirmative action is strictly limited under the law. Affirmative action is lawful under Title VII when it is **designed to respond to a demonstrated and serious imbalance in traditionally segregated job categories; is flexible, time-limited, applies only to qualified workers; and respects the rights of non-minorities and men.**

- Affirmative action, when properly designed and implemented, **does not** allow for the use of **quotas** -- the inflexible reliance solely on numbers which ignores qualification -- which has **never** been lawful.

- As a federal enforcement agency, the EEOC supports affirmative action programs that are consistent with the law. The Commission views such programs as a limited, but important, tool in the fight to eradicate discrimination.

Types of Affirmative Action

There are two kinds of affirmative action -- **voluntary** and **court-ordered**. The following sets out the Title VII standards governing each type of affirmative action.

Courtesy of the U.S. Equal Employment Opportunity Commission.

Voluntary Affirmative Action

- Voluntary affirmative action plans are valid under Title VII if they meet the standards established by the Supreme Court in *Johnson v. Transportation Agency, Santa Clara County, California*, 480 U.S. 616, 42 EPD ¶ 36,831 (1987), and *United Steel Workers v. Weber*, 443 U.S. 193, 20 EPD ¶ 30,026 (1979).

- Under *Johnson* and *Weber*, an employer can adopt a voluntary affirmative action plan if it identifies a **manifest imbalance in traditionally segregated job categories**. The plan must be designed to break down patterns of segregation and to open employment opportunities for the targeted group, usually minorities or women, in jobs from which they have traditionally been barred.

- **Second**, a voluntary affirmative action plan **cannot unnecessarily trammel the rights of non-targeted groups, usually non-minorities** or **men**. For example, such a plan cannot require the discharge of non-targeted employees and their replacement with targeted employees nor can it create an absolute bar to the advancement of non-targeted employees.

  Applicable law also requires that an individual who benefits from affirmative action **must be qualified for the job** at issue, although that individual need not be the **most** qualified individual.

- **Finally**, a voluntary affirmative action plan **must be temporary and flexible** and it cannot be used to **maintain** a balanced workforce. A voluntary plan should be regularly reviewed to ensure that any **goals and timetables** are justified and flexible and that the rights of non-targeted groups are not unduly burdened.

- Affirmative action implemented by federal, state or local government employers must be narrowly tailored to further compelling governmental interests.

Remedial or Court-Ordered Affirmative Action

- Courts can order affirmative action to remedy proven discrimination. Such remedies have been ordered particularly in cases where (1) it is impossible to identify the actual victims of discrimination under Title VII, and (2) this remedy is necessary to further the goals of Title VII to eliminate employment discrimination.

- Court-ordered affirmative action is subject to stricter standards than voluntary affirmative action. The Supreme Court set out the Title VII requirements for court-ordered affirmative action in *Local 28 of Sheet Metal Workers v. EEOC*, 478 U.S. 421 (1986).

2

<u>Remedial or Court-Ordered Affirmative Action</u> -- cont.

- Court-ordered affirmative action is appropriate under Title VII **only** where there is proof of pervasive and systemic discrimination (a higher burden of proof than is required for voluntary plans).

- Court-ordered affirmative action must be **narrowly tailored, flexible and temporary, and it cannot impose an unacceptable burden on non-targeted groups, usually non-minorities or men.**

<u>The EEOC's Guidelines on Affirmative Action</u>

- The EEOC issued its **Guidelines on Affirmative Action,** 29 C.F.R. Part 1608, in 1979, and they are entirely consistent with the parameters of affirmative action established by the Supreme Court in *Johnson* and *Weber*. The Guidelines remained intact through both the Reagan and Bush administrations, and continue to be in effect.

- The Guidelines are intended simply to clarify or explain applicable law. They **do not** impose additional requirements or standards for employers.

- The Guidelines anticipate: (1) that an employer will identify a manifest imbalance in its workforce before voluntarily undertaking affirmative action or the employer's actions will not be justified; (2) that the goals and timetables adopted by the employer must be flexible and temporary; and (3) that the employer must ensure that the rights of non-targeted groups are not unnecessarily burdened by the voluntary affirmative action plan.

Recent Developments

- Two recent events have affected affirmative action in employment: the June 1995 Supreme Court ruling in the case of *Adarand Constructors, Inc. v. Pena* and a July 1995 Presidential Directive on affirmative action issued by President Clinton. Both reaffirmed that affirmative action programs, when properly applied, are still an appropriate tool to redress discrimination and provide for equal employment opportunity.

<u>Adarand v. Pena</u>

- On June 12, 1995, in its opinion in *Adarand Constructors, Inc. v. Pena*, 115 S. Ct. 2097 (1995), the Supreme Court tightened the standards under which federal government agencies can use race-based preferences to award procurement contracts. The ruling did **not** abolish federal affirmative action programs. Rather, the Court held that affirmative action programs at the federal level **must** meet the same standard imposed on states in the ruling *Richmond v. J.A. Croson Co.*, 488 U.S. 469 (1989). Under the *Croson* standard, federal race based programs "must serve a compelling governmental interest, and must be narrowly tailored to further that interest."

3

Adarand v. Pena -- cont.

- In the *Adarand* ruling, the Court stated: "Government is not disqualified from acting in response to the unhappy persistence of both the practice and the lingering effects of racial discrimination against minority groups in this country." However, the Court mandated that federal affirmative action programs will "be subjected to detailed judicial inquiry to ensure that the personal right to equal protection of the law has not been infringed."

- The *Adarand* ruling does **not** address private sector, voluntary affirmative action plans.

Presidential Directive

- On July 19, 1995, President Clinton announced the results of an in-depth White House task force study of federal affirmative action programs. The President concluded that affirmative action, when properly conducted, "has been good for America."

- The President issued a Directive to the heads of all federal agencies requiring them to assess their affirmative action programs to meet the new strict standards imposed by the *Adarand* ruling and to ensure that affirmative action programs are fair and consistent with the ideals of personal responsibility and merit.

- According to the Directive, any affirmative action program must be changed or eliminated if it fails to meet the following four principles:

  o   No quotas.
  o   No reverse discrimination.
  o   No preferences for unqualified individuals.
  o   No continuation of programs that have met their goals.

- It is the position of the Administration that affirmative action, when consistent with *Adarand* and the Presidential Directive, should continue to be an effective tool to promote equal employment opportunity in America.

Prepared by
EEOC Office of Communications and Legislative Affairs
(revised March 1996)

Hate crimes, as defined by the Federal Bureau of Investigation (FBI), are crimes "motivated by the offender's bias against the victim's religion, race, ethnicity, or sexual orientation." The U.S. law enforcement community recognizes that bias-motivated crimes, or hate crimes, are neither new to humankind nor unique to America. Moreover, the nature of the crimes makes them difficult to combat. The FBI believes that the collection of valid data concerning these crimes is requisite to addressing them.

To implement the Hate Crime Statistics Act of 1990, the FBI-sponsored Uniform Crime Reporting Program developed a data-collection system that receives information from city, county, and state law enforcement agencies. The following table is from *Hate Crime Statistics 1994*, published by the Criminal Justice Information Services (CJIS) division of the FBI. According to the CJIS, the data compiled are provided by 7,356 law enforcement agencies responsible for approximately 58 percent of the U.S. population.

Table 1. - Number of Incidents, Offenses, Victims, and Offenders by Bias Motivation, 1994

	Number of			
	Incidents	Offenses	Victims	Known Offenders
Total	**5,932**	**7,262**	**7,498**	**6,265**
Bias Motivation				
Race:	**3,545**	**4,431**	**4,540**	**4,356**
Anti-White	1,010	1,269	1,314	1,794
Anti-Black	2,174	2,693	2,739	2,149
Anti-American Indian/				
Alaskan Native	22	24	24	30
Anti-Asian/Pacific Islander	211	269	280	252
Anti-Multi-Racial Group	128	176	183	131
Ethnicity/National Origin:	**638**	**790**	**840**	**717**
Anti-Hispanic	337	446	471	468
Anti-Other Ethnicity/				
National Origin	301	344	369	249
Religion:	**1,062**	**1,244**	**1,305**	**415**
Anti-Jewish	915	1,088	1,134	353
Anti-Catholic	17	19	20	11
Anti-Protestant	29	31	40	6
Anti-Islamic	17	17	17	4
Anti-Other Religious Group	67	72	77	37
Anti-Multi-Religious Group	14	14	14	3
Anti-Atheism/Agnosticism/etc.	3	3	3	1
Sexual Orientation:	**685**	**793**	**809**	**775**
Anti-Male Homosexual	501	567	580	616
Anti-Female Homosexual	100	121	121	87
Anti-Homosexual	63	79	82	54
Anti-Heterosexual	14	16	16	13
Anti-Bisexual	7	10	10	5
Multiple Bias:	**2**	**4**	**4**	**2**

Courtesy of the Criminal Justice Information Services, Federal Bureau of Investigation.

POLITICAL SOCIALIZATION AND PARTICIPATION

11   KidsVention '96, World Wide Web Site

American children learn about the ideas and processes of democracy while growing up in a democratic environment. The project presented here tries to augment that experience. Posted on the World Wide Web by the Kids Voting San Jose/Silicon Valley Student Advisory Committee, KidsVention '96 is fascinating and engaging: High school students are invited to debate and vote on three issues—one federal, one state, and one local—on the Web. Two hundred and sixteen local schools have participated in the project. Here is part of the debate over the local issue: whether Santa Clara County should mandate school uniforms as a way to provide a positive learning environment.

Resolutions for KidsVention '96

The following three issues were selected by the KidsVoting San José / Silicon Valley Student Advisory Committee. This committee is made up entirely of middle school and high school students and has an adult moderator. All decisions made by this committee come from student generated ideas and student voting.

These resolutions will be debated by high school students at KidsVention. Students at the event will then vote electronically while those participating on the KidsVention webpage will be able to vote via the web page.

Select an issue:

Federal :|: **State** :|: **Local** :|: **Sponsors**

REGISTER NOW
You must register before Voting !

 GO TO BALLOT

VOTE NOW

KidsVoting Home

World Wide WebPort

Courtesy of the Internet WWW site of the Kids Voting San Jose/Silicon Valley Student Advisory Committee.

Resolved:

Santa Clara County should provide a positive learning environment by instituting a compulsory plan for uniforms in public schools.

--LOCAL--

Summary

This Resolution Proposes that public schools in the Santa Clara County Mandate school uniforms as a way to provide a positive learning environment.

What A YES Vote Means

A **YES** on this resolution means: County public school children would have to comply with a county wide uniform policy. This will elimminate gang recogniton during class hours.

What A NO Vote Means

A **NO** on this resolution means: County School children will continue to choose what they wear to school on a daily basis. And the first ammendment right of free expression will continue to be protected.

Arguments Pro

Presently Gang violence in school is ever present. Local school districts should take action to ensure that schools remain a place where a positive learning environment can be found. Since the education of our youth is a primary concern, this resolution will save lives and enhance education.

Arguments Con

The Santa Clara County is a melting pot of different cultures. A mandatory uniform policy denies the student the opportunity to use traditional dress as a representation of their indiviidual heritage. It also infringes on the first amendment right of free expression.

 KIDS VOTING | EXPRESS YOURSELF | VIEW MOST RECENT

On 3/19/1996 at 8:36 , **Jessica Aviles** in San Jose said:
I feel children should not have to wear uniforms. If people are going to be in gangs then they will. Whether they wear a uniform or not. It doesn't make a difference, people are going to do what they want when they want. Personally, I have been wearing a uniform all of my life and it's not going to change a thing.

On 3/19/1996 at 8:40 , **Adriane Vane** in San Jose said:
I think that all students should wear a uniform because it stops a lot of competition during school.
I have worn a uniform all of my life and it is so much easier because than I don't have to impress anyone with my clothes and they learned to like me for who I really am.

On 3/19/1996 at 8:46 , **Danielle Orsua** in San Jose said:
I think that public school students should wear uniforms because it helps to set an example of what they represent. What does it look like now, students wearing baggy pants and gross clothes, when they could look nice and clean and normal.

On 3/19/1996 at 8:47 , **Addie Vane** in San Jose said:
I am cool!

12   Project Vote Smart, World Wide Web Site

For the 1996 elections, many voter education projects were posted on the Internet. With cochairmen former U.S. presidents Jimmy Carter and Gerald Ford, Project Vote Smart is a nonprofit, nonpartisan organization. Endeavoring to increase political participation in the United States, the primary function of Project Vote Smart is to provide voters "with information about the political system, issues, candidates and elected officials." Operated at Oregon State University in Corvallis, Oregon, and Northeastern University in Boston, Massachusetts, its Web site was updated every day during the 1996 election campaign with comprehensive and independent information on biographical history, voting records, campaign finances, and the campaign promises of candidates for public office at all levels of government.

"It's Time to Hire the Help"

Welcome to the *Vote Smart Web*, your one-stop shopping center for political information. This service, which links **Project Vote Smart**'s unique database with other sources found on the Internet, is researcher assisted. If you have any trouble sorting through the maze of political information available, our researchers can direct you to what you are looking for. Call us free of charge at:

1-800-622-SMART

What's New:

1996 State Legislative Races:

* California, Illinois, Ohio, Texas

Biographical and Contact Information for State Legislators

Your Government

Federal Government Information

* The President and the Executive Branch
* Congress
  * Data from Project Vote Smart
* The Judiciary

State Government Information

* Organized By State
* Organized By Category

Courtesy of the Internet WWW site of Project Vote Smart.

Political Campaigns

- 1996 Campaigns & Elections
  - The 1996 Presidential Campaign
    - Candidate Information from Project Vote Smart

- 1995 Elections

Issue Information

Organizations Related to Politics

Educational and Reference Resources

- Historical Documents
- How the US Government Works -- An Introduction
- Online Political News Sources
- Political Resources, Research, and Statistics

Miscellaneous Political Resources

- Political Humor
- Political Audio Clips on the Internet
- Images of Politics and Government on the Internet
- Links Where You Can Participate

Other Directories of Political Information

What is Project Vote Smart?

Project Vote Smart is a voter's self-defense system that provides voters with factual information on candidates and elected officials. For more detailed information:

- Background and History
- Current Press Releases
- How to Become a Member
- Our Publications
- Job Openings at Project Vote Smart

Disclaimer

Project Vote Smart scrupulously researches and conducts numerous checks on all of the information in our own database. However, we link to many other independent sources of information on the World Wide Web in an attempt to offer you a one-stop-shopping site for political information.

While we stand by the accuracy of our own database, we can not vouch for the accuracy of the information from other sites. Should you find misinformation at any of the sites to which we link, please contact the site in question and also let us know.

Permission to Use Project Vote Smart Data

Project Vote Smart does NOT copyright any of its publications or databases. We do this so that citizens, schools, libraries, and other users may copy and distribute the information freely.

The Project encourages citizens to share the abundant, accurate information that we assemble and feel is essential to successful self-governance.

Should you copy and distribute information from our publications or databases please do so in context and attribute the information to Project Vote Smart.

Please contact Project Vote Smart's Director of Public Information, Adelaide Elm, at (541) 754-2746 (e-mail: aelm@vote-smart.org) with any questions regarding the use of Project Vote Smart material.

Thank you for your cooperation!

Vote Smart Web is a new and evolving service. The interns and volunteers at Project Vote Smart are working hard to collect as much political information as possible for you. Please let us know what you think by using the forms below.

Send Us Your Comments   *Suggest a Link*   *Request Printed Information*

6

PUBLIC OPINION

13   A Gallup Poll

In each presidential election year, almost all public opinion polls or surveys ask this type of question: What do you think is the most important problem facing this nation today? During the primary season in 1996, based on its poll, the Gallup Poll came to the following conclusion: In the 1996 presidential campaign, the most important issues that concerned Americans were Medicare and the federal budget. Founded by George Gallup in the 1930s, the Gallup Poll is a renowned institution which conducts public opinion polls worldwide.

Most Important Issues In Presidential Campaign: Medicare, Budget

By David W. Moore

In a hypothetical presidential race between Bill Clinton and Bob Dole, the issues of Medicare, the budget deficit and the economy do the best job of explaining the public's vote, according to a recent Gallup poll. The crime issue plays only a small role in determining the vote, while education and health care play virtually no role. Yet a separate Gallup poll shows that in the abstract, Americans identify education and crime as top priority issues for the presidential campaign, followed closely by the economy and health care. This discrepancy between the issues that people *say* are most important and the issues that influence how they actually vote suggests that education, health care and especially crime could become significant factors in the election, even though they have little influence now.

Typically, pollsters evaluate the importance of issues in one of two ways. One is to ask people to rate the importance of the issues, and the other is to measure how well people's positions on the issues predict, or correlate with, their vote choice. But the two ways do not necessarily lead to similar conclusions.

In two January Gallup polls, for example, 44 percent of the public rated education as the "top priority" issue that would determine their vote for president, the highest number for any issue. Yet the statistical analysis shows that voters who rate Dole higher than Clinton on the issue of education are not more likely to vote for Dole. Thus, knowing a voter's ratings of the two candidates on the issue of education does not predict which candidate that person will choose. On the other hand, voters who rate Dole higher than Clinton on the budget deficit *are* more likely to vote for Dole, and by a significant margin. In this case, knowing a voter's ratings of the two candidates on the budget deficit does help predict which candidate the voter will choose.

Overall, when Americans are asked to rate the issues they say will affect their vote for president, the poll shows that more people mention education (44 percent) and crime (41 percent) as their "top priority" than any other issues. The economy (37 percent) and health care (37 percent) are close behind.

Medicare Best Predictor

When it comes down to choosing between Clinton and Dole, however, the poll shows that voters do not base their decisions on how these candidates are handling education or health care. A statistical analysis reveals that the public's ratings of the candidates on Medicare constitute the most important predictor of their vote choice, followed closely by the budget deficit and the economy. Crime and taxes are mildly important predictors, while education and health care have virtually no influence on the public's vote.

One reason why education and health care are not now important predictors of the public's vote, despite their high priority ratings, is that those issues have not received a great deal of media attention in recent weeks. Since November, the news media have focused much of their coverage on the budget impasse between the Republican Congress and President Clinton, which includes the conflict over Medicare and the implications of this standoff for the economy. Thus, it is not surprising that at this stage of the campaign those three issues exert the strongest influence on the public's vote choice. The crime bill and taxes have been mentioned in the press, and they do exert some influence on the vote, but not nearly as much as the three top issues.

The high priority the public says it places on education, health care and crime suggests that although these issues are not currently important, they could be "sleepers" – emerging as major issues later in the campaign. ☑

Next, I'm going to read a list which includes some national issues and some problems facing Americans today. For each one, please tell me how important a candidate's position on
that issue is to you personally in deciding which candidate you will support for president.
First, would you say [item] is a top priority in how you vote, a high priority in how you vote,
very important but not a priority, somewhat important, or not important? (RANDOM ORDER)

Priority Issues in Determining Vote

	Priority		Not priority			
	Top	High	Very important	Somewhat important	Not important	No opinion
The quality of education in public schools through grade 12	44%	23	25	5	2	1
The rate of violent crime in the United States	41%	25	24	8	1	1
The nation's economy	37%	27	26	7	1	2
The availability of health care coverage in the U.S.	37%	26	26	8	2	1
The cost of health care in the U.S.	36%	27	26	9	1	1
The availability of good jobs in the U.S.	35%	28	27	7	2	1
The problem of drug abuse in the U.S.	35%	23	28	11	3	•
The federal budget deficit	33%	25	26	11	3	2
The nation's moral values	33%	22	26	12	5	2
Financial security for people once they retire	31%	27	29	9	3	1
Medicare policy	29%	26	30	12	2	1
The amount Americans pay in federal taxes	29%	23	31	12	4	1
The level of poverty in the U.S.	27%	24	32	13	3	1
Welfare policy	26%	23	28	16	5	2
The cost of college education	21%	22	31	17	7	2
The size and role of the federal government	20%	21	31	19	6	3
America's role in world affairs	14%	20	32	25	7	2

• Less than 0.5%

Campaign '96: The Voters' Priority Issues (January 5-7, 1996; Survey GP 9601001 [GO 105814], Q. 14.)
(percent rating top or high priority)

QUESTION: I'm going to read a list which includes some national issues and some problems facing Americans today. For each one, please tell me how important a candidate's position on that issue is to you personally in deciding which candidate you will support for president. First, would you say [item] is a top priority in how you vote, a high priority in how you vote, very important but not a priority, somewhat important, or not important? (RANDOM ORDER)

	Quality of public education	Rate of violent crime	The economy	Availability of health care coverage	Health care costs	Availability of good jobs	No. of interviews
National	67%	66%	64%	63%	63%	63%	1000
Sex							
Male	61	63	65	57	57	61	497
Female	73	69	63	68	68	65	503
Age							
18-29 years	74	70	67	63	64	69	193
30-49 years	71	67	67	65	62	68	448
50-64 years	61	59	66	62	65	58	199
65 & older	60	69	62	58	63	51	151
Region							
East	69	63	65	66	64	66	242
Midwest	66	69	60	59	59	60	259
South	69	67	66	64	65	62	311
West	65	65	67	64	63	65	188
Community							
Urban	63	66	66	64	63	68	402
Suburban	67	60	66	63	63	59	354
Rural	70	66	58	60	62	63	236
Race							
White	68	66	65	64	63	63	831
Non-white	60	70	63	61	61	67	159
Education							
College postgraduate	64	51	63	58	54	56	162
Bachelor's degree only	70	59	67	53	60	57	157
Some college	69	68	66	66	65	64	291
High school or less	67	72	64	65	65	64	386
Politics							
Republicans	66	64	64	62	57	59	337
Democrats	71	70	68	75	69	71	283
Independents	67	65	62	63	64	60	380
Ideology							
Liberal	71	64	66	72	71	68	173
Moderate	63	67	62	66	63	56	363
Conservative	69	68	66	57	60	61	427
Clinton approval							
Approve	67	67	64	73	69	67	499
Disapprove	70	67	66	55	58	60	422
Income							
$75,000 & over	74	62	48	68	53	54	143
$50,000 & over	69	60	69	58	58	58	317
$30,000-49,999	70	63	69	60	62	68	255
$20,000-29,999	64	73	67	77	74	67	152
Under $20,000	69	70	56	60	61	65	222

Summary of 1996 Campaign Issues

	Is priority	Is not
Very high		
1. Education	67%	33
2. Crime	66%	34
3. The economy	64%	36
4. Health care coverage	63%	37
5. Health care costs	63%	37
6. Jobs	63%	37
Moderately high		
7. Drug abuse	58%	42
8. Federal deficit	58%	42
9. Retirement security	58%	42
10. Moral values	55%	45
11. Medicare policy	55%	45
Mixed		
12. Amount of taxes	52%	48
13. Poverty levels	51%	49
14. Welfare policy	49%	51
Low		
15. College costs	43%	57
16. Scope of federal government	41%	59
17. Role in world	34%	66

With the robust growth of the Internet population, the number of online opinion surveys has been increasing rapidly. This Term Limits Survey is conducted by the Term Limits Leadership Council on the World Wide Web. The Council is a coalition of state-based groups advocating term limits for elected officials. The survey seeks to determine whether computer-literate Americans think differently from the general public about congressional term limits, and if so, what the difference is.

Back to: ◉ Home Page ▨ Front Page ◉ TLLC

TERM LIMITS LEADERSHIP COUNCIL
2915 Providence Road, Suite 300, Charlotte, North Carolina 28211
Phone 1-800-554-6487 Fax 1-704-365-0615

3 Terms in the House
2 in the Senate

A coalition of state-based term limit groups that believes Congress has a clear conflict of interest on term limits

Scott W. Rasmussen, Chairman
www.termlimits.org

Term Limits Survey

opinion of 1,000 adult voters, conducted by Fabrizio-McLaughlin & Assoc.
for Term Limits Leadership Council Jan. 15-18, 1996, +/- 3.1%

Are you interested in voter opinion in America on the most important questions to the congressional term limits movement? Then answer the following four questions, worded exactly as asked in the recent Fabrizio-McLaughlin & Assoc. national survey.

By including your **name and email address** you will receive the results of the national survey as a confirmation after submitting ... compare **your** answers to America's!

email: [   ]
First name: [   ] Last name: [   ]

(**Note**: If you are unable to change an answer, set your browser wider.)

Courtesy of the WWW site of Fabrizio-McLaughlin & Associates.

1. Do you favor or oppose limiting the number of terms that members of Congress can serve?

○ Strongly Favor
○ Somewhat Favor
○ Somewhat Oppose
○ Strongly Oppose
○ Don't Know / No Answer

2. Under the current law, members of Congress serve for 2-year terms. If you were to limit the number of terms a member of Congress could serve, would you prefer to make it three terms which is six years or six terms, which is 12 years?

○ 3 terms (six years)
○ 6 terms (twelve years)
○ Don't Know / No Answer

3. Suppose that two candidates for Congress both promise to vote for term limits. One candidate pledges to voluntarily serve no more than three terms in Congress, whether or not term limits become law. The other candidate refuses to limit the number of terms he would serve in Congress. All other things being equal, who would you be more likely to vote for, the candidate who:

○ Limits own terms
○ Refuses to limit own terms
○ It makes no difference
○ Don't Know / No Answer

4. Suppose that two candidates running for Congress in your district both promise to vote for term limits if elected. One candidate promises to vote for limits of three (3) terms in the House, the other promises to vote for limits of six (6) terms in the House. All other things being equal, who would you be more likely to vote for, the candidate who promises to vote for term limits of:

○ Three (3) terms
○ Six (6) terms
○ It makes no difference
○ Don't Know / No Answer

Comment area:

```
                                                                    ▲



                                                                    ▼
◄                                                                   ►
```

What? You don't want the interactivity? OK. Then just read "Living and Dying by Term Limits", Paul Jacob's Op-Ed from **The Washington Times**, Mar. 14; a commentary on the results of this survey.

| Submit Response & Receive Results | Clear All Fields |

○ Send me a 3-month complimentary subscription to **U.S. Term Limits'** newsletter **"No Uncertain Terms"**

○ I want to make a $15 sponsor contribution and receive the newsletter year-round

○ Put me on your media contact list

email: [_____] First Name: [_____] Last Name: [_____]

Street Address [_____] City [_____] State

[___] Zip [_____]

[Submit this request] (please include mailing address for **"No Uncertain Terms"**)

[Clear all info]

Your comments & suggestions are welcomed!

This page was designed by admin@termlimits.org Wednesday, 10-Jul-96 13:27:11 PDT and has been accessed 1080 times since this counter was added. © 1996 Paul R. Farago

15   Publications of Two Interest Groups: Common Cause and the AFL-CIO

Here are descriptions of two interest groups written in their own words. The organizations are: Common Cause, a public interest group, and the AFL-CIO, a labor union. The description of Common Cause is an excerpt from its leaflet, while that of the AFL-CIO is from the union's World Wide Web site.

Common Cause

1250 CONNECTICUT AVENUE, NW ◆ WASHINGTON, D.C. 20036 ◆ PHONE: (202) 833-1200 ◆ FAX: (202) 659-3716

EDWARD S. CABOT	ANN McBRIDE	ARCHIBALD COX	JOHN GARDNER
Chairman	*President*	*Chairman Emeritus*	*Founding Chairman*

"Common Cause ... has been an uncommonly successful lobby ... in terms of the depth and breadth of its efforts -- in the Congress and state legislatures -- there probably has never been a reform movement so active and with such a record of accomplishment."
-- Christian Science Monitor

"When the little guy wins, it's likely that Common Cause had something to do with the victory. It's good to know that the people can make a difference."
-- St. Petersburg Times

Common Cause was founded in 1970 by John Gardner, former Secretary of Health, Education and Welfare, as a nonpartisan citizens' lobbying group. His idea -- to bring together individuals from across the nation in an effort to lobby elected officials on national issues of mutual concern.

Common Cause was to be financed by the dues and contributions of the individuals who joined as members. And its effectiveness was to be drawn from the focused and concerted grassroots lobbying activities of its members around the country, combined with professional lobbying on Capitol Hill.

Within a year, more than 100,000 citizens joined Common Cause, and its agenda quickly grew to include ending U.S. involvement in Vietnam, reforming the campaign finance system, and pressing for civil rights, ethics, financial and lobby disclosure and open meeting laws.

In recognition of the need for fundamental reform at the state level as well, Common Cause soon began organizing parallel lobbying efforts in the states and establishing Common Cause state organizations.

Courtesy of Common Cause and the AFL-CIO.

AFL-CIO Welcome Message

The AFL-CIO is a federation of 78 labor unions representing some 13.6 million working men and women who have joined together to help workers improve their lives on the job and in their communities.

Through organizing, collective bargaining and legislative/political action, the unions of the AFL-CIO work to advance and defend the rights of working people everywhere.

In this century, the labor movement has been the author of America's quality of life by organizing workers, building their ladder into the middle class, and creating a market based on good wages and conditions that is the envy of the world.

As a new century dawns, and working people find themselves under harsh attack from the agents of the privileged, the unions of the AFL-CIO are determined to continue our struggle for economic and social justice -- at home and abroad -- and for the dignity of every working family.

We will win because we will not quit!

A special welcome to AFL-CIO LaborNET subscribers!!!

If you are a union member and would like to find out more about subscribing to the AFL-CIO's LaborNET on CompuServe, click here.

We hope you enjoy your visit to the AFL-CIO Home Page on the World Wide Web.

16 Lobbying on the Internet by the UAW: The Minimum Wage Act

For the United Auto Workers (UAW) membership, "Action Alert" is the slogan of its grassroots lobbying page on the Internet. The UAW leadership has targeted U.S. senators' endorsement of the Democratic party version of the Minimum Wage Act 1996. At the end of this action proclamation, the word *Senators* is a hyperlink to an E-mail address directory of U.S. senators.

Many labor unions have adopted similar grassroots lobbying strategies on their Web sites and use the "Action Alert" slogan. These labor union Internet sites can be an influential part of a successful lobbying effort: The U.S. Senate passed the Minimum Wage Act of 1996 without Republican senator Kit Bond's amendment, which would have exempted small businesses from the minimum-wage mandate. President Clinton signed the bill into law in August 1996.

ACTION ALERT!

→Senate Will Vote on Minimum Wage July 9

Now's the Time to Tell Your Senators How You Feel!

With the Senate vote on July 9, we'll know whether America's most underpaid workers will finally get the raise most Americans believe they deserve.

Courtesy of the United Auto Workers' WWW site on the Internet.

The UAW and other unions are pressing for an up-or-down vote on a clean bill to provide a long-overdue increase in the minimum wage. But Republican leaders are pushing an amendment by Senator Kit Bond which would exempt about 10 million workers at small businesses from getting the raise. This gutting amendment would set a permanent subminimum wage for people employed by small businesses. Please act now to urge your Senators to vote against this Bond amendment. Insist that they pass a clean minimum wage bill, without any gimmicks or weakening amendments.

The bill also includes tax changes -- including rolling back all taxes workers pay on tuition refund and other educational benefits they get from employers. Those benefits were tax-free until this Congress failed to renew the tax exemption -- which would now be extended to the end of the year.

Nine out of ten Americans think that today's minimum wage -- which is still stuck at $4.25 an hour -- is too low and should be boosted by at least 90 cents an hour. That would directly help 12 million workers earn a decent living -- and indirectly help millions more, whose wage scales are linked to the minimum. Today's minimum wage leaves full-time workers getting just $8,800 a year --$3,000 less than the poverty line for a family of three.

Although Republican leaders tried to block a minimum wage hike in both houses of Congress, popular outrage finally forced the House of Representatives to approve a raise on May 23 totaling 90 cents, hiking the minimum to $5.15 an hour by July, 1997. Although not many union members have to work at the minimum wage, the labor movement alerted the public to how Senator Bob Dole and Rep. Newt Gingrich were trying keep Congress from even voting on the raise, and we're lobbying hard for passage.

The House had defeated a Republican move to carve out a huge loophole for small business after 43 Republicans broke from their leadership and joined most Democrats in voting for a raise without crippling loopholes. Democrats voted against the loophole 185 to 7, while 189 Republicans backed it.

In the Senate Bob Dole had blocked the raise for weeks by trying to merge it into the anti-worker "TEAM" Act (S. 295). (The TEAM Act would, for the first time in sixty years, give companies a green light to set up sham "unions" directly controlled by management. It would make a mockery of workers' democratic rights to elect their own leaders.) The Senate finally agreed to vote on the minimum wage July 9, and then on the 9th or 10th, vote on the "TEAM" Act separately.

➡How you can make a difference:

Please act now. Contact your Senators and let them know that you care, and you won't accept anti-worker substitutes. We want them to finally raise the minimum wage -- without crippling amendments. Or call them at the UAW's special toll-free number: 1-800-962-3524.

This sample letter is presented on the Internet by the National Rifle Association (NRA) to its membership. According to an NRA directive, a constituent's letter to an elected Capitol Hill official is "a time-tested, results-oriented method" to influence pending legislation. It is "an easy way for you to let your lawmakers know your views on specific issues, encourage them to vote your way, and let them know you'll watch how they vote on a particular issue and keep that vote in mind come Election Day!" Further, "Lawmakers often calculate that each letter they receive represents the similar views of 500 other constituents."

SAMPLE LETTER TO LAWMAKERS

Your Name
Address
City, State, Zip

Date

The Honorable _____
United States House of Representatives
Washington, D.C. 20515

Dear Representative _____:

As someone who lives and votes in your district, I strongly urge you to oppose any additional "gun control" proposals that may be debated in the U.S. Congress. Instead, I urge you to support legislation that focuses on real crime control and keeping violent criminals off our streets.

Restrictive gun laws have been ineffective to date because they are aimed at guns and the law-abiding citizens who own or want to own them, rather than at the core problem: criminals. Everything from waiting periods to registration to licensing to outright bans of certain firearms has been tried to no avail for a simple reason: criminals by definition are law breakers who do not and will not abide by these laws. Criminals need to be the focus of any crime control measure because the overwhelming majority of all violent crime in this country is committed by previously convicted repeat felons.

In closing, I again encourage you to concentrate your efforts on crime control, not gun control. Support efforts to reform our ailing criminal justice system and keep violent offenders behind bars. I thank you for your time, and would appreciate it if you would inform me of your position on our Second Amendment rights and effective "crime control."

Sincerely,

Your Name

Courtesy of the National Rifle Association's WWW site.

18   The Republican Party Platform

To define their messages and publicize their stands on the major issues, political parties periodically develop platforms. Usually in the form of a booklet, the platforms are distributed by the parties to the press and public. Excerpted here is part of the platform of the Republican party, released at the party's convention in August 1996.

Document of the Republican party.

PREAMBLE

We meet to nominate a candidate and pass a platform at a moment of measureless national opportunity. A new century beckons, and Americans are more than equal to its challenges. But there is a problem. The Clinton administration has proven unequal to the heritage of our past, the promise of our times, and the character of the American people. They require more and demand better. With them, we raise our voices and raise our sights.

We are the heirs of world leadership that was earned by bravery and sacrifice on half a thousand battlefields. We will soon nominate for the presidency a man who knew battle and so loves peace, a man who lives bravely and so walks humbly with his God and his fellow citizens. We walk with him now as he joins one more battle, every bit as crucial for our country's future as was the crusade in which he served.

Just when America should be leading the world, we have an administration squandering the international respect it did not earn and does not value. Just when America should be demonstrating anew the dynamic power of economic freedom, we have an administration working against both history and public opinion to expand the reach and burden of government. Just when Americans are reasserting their deepest values, we have an administration locked into the counterculture battles of its youth.

Americans are right to say we are on the wrong track. Our prestige in the world is declining. Economic growth here at home is anemic. Our society grows more violent and less decent. The only way the Clinton administration can magnify its questionable accomplishments is to lower our expectations. Those who lead the Democrat party call America to smaller tasks and downsized dreams.

That is not the calling of an American president.

Today's Democrat leaders do not understand leadership. They reduce principles to tactics. They talk endlessly and confront nothing. They offer, not convictions, but alibis. They are paralyzed by indecision, weakened by scandal and guided only by the perpetuation of their own power.

We asked for change. We worked for reform. We offered cooperation and consensus. Now, the asking is over. The Clinton administration cannot be reinvented, it must be replaced.

Republicans do not duplicate or fabricate or counterfeit a vision for the land we love. With our fellow citizens, we assert the present power of timeless truths.

This is what we want for America: real prosperity that reaches beyond the stock market to every family, small business and worker. An economy expanding as fast as American enterprise and creativity will carry it, free from unnecessary taxes, regulation and litigation.

1

This is what we want for America: the restoration of self-government by breaking Washington's monopoly on power. The American people want their country back. We will help them to regain it.

This too we want for America: moral clarity in our culture and ethical leadership in the White House. We offer America, not a harsh moralism, but our sincere conviction that the values we hold in our hearts determine the success of our lives and the shape of our society. It matters greatly that our leaders reflect and communicate those values, not undermine or mock them.

The diversity of our nation is reflected in this platform. We ask for the support and participation of all who substantially share our agenda. In one way or another, every Republican is a dissenter. At the same time, we are not morally indifferent. In this, as in many things, Lincoln is our model. At a time of great crisis, he spoke both words of healing and words of conviction. We do likewise, not for the peace of a political party, but because we citizens are bound together in a great enterprise for our children's future.

The platform that follows marshals these principles and sends them into action. We aim at nothing less than an economy of dynamic growth; a renewal of community, self-government and citizenship; and a national reaffirmation of the enduring principles on which America's greatness depends. We will count our victories, not in elections won or in economic numbers on a chart, but in the everyday achievements of the American dream: when a man or woman discovers the dignity and confidence of a job; when a child rejects drugs and embraces life; when an entrepreneur turns an idea into an industry; when a family once again feels the security of its savings and has control over the education of its children.

None of the extraordinary things about our country are gifts of government. They are the accomplishments of free people in a free society. They are achievements, not entitlements — and are sweeter for that fact. They result when men and women live in obedience to their conscience, not to the state. All our efforts as Republicans are guided by the fixed star of this single principle: that freedom always exceeds our highest expectations.

This is the greatest task before the Republican Party: to raise the bar of American expectations. Of the potential of our economy. Of the order and civility of our culture. Of what a president can be, and what the presidency must be again.

There is a continuing revolution in the yellowed parchment and faded ink of the American creed...a revolution that will long outlive us. It can carry the weight of all our hopes. It can reward every dreamer. It is the reason that America's finest hour is never a memory and always a goal.

With trust in God and in fidelity to generations past and generations to come, we respectfully submit this platform to the American people.

2

PRINCIPLES OF THE 1996 REPUBLICAN PLATFORM

Introduction

Because Americans are a diverse and tolerant people, they have differences of opinion on many issues. But as a people, we share a common dream and common goals:

A strong America that protects its citizens and champions their democratic ideals throughout the world,

An America with a vibrant and growing economy that improves the standard of living for all,

An America with a smaller, more effective and less intrusive government that trusts its people to decide what is best for them,

An America whose people feel safe and secure in their homes, on their streets, and in their communities,

An America where our children receive the best education in the world and learn the values like decency and responsibility that made this country great,

And an America with the compassion to care for those who cannot care for themselves.

Principles

1. Because the American Dream fulfills the promise of liberty, we believe it should be attainable by all through more and secure jobs, home ownership, personal security, and education that meets the challenges of the century ahead.

2. Because a dynamic and growing economy is the best way to create more and better paying jobs, with greater security in the work place, we believe in lower taxes within a simpler tax system, in tandem with fair and open trade and a balanced federal budget.

3. Because wasteful government spending and over-regulation, fueled by higher taxes, are the greatest obstacles to job creation and economic growth, we believe in a Balanced Budget Amendment to the Constitution and a common-sense approach to government rules and red tape.

4. Because we recognize our obligation to foster hope and opportunity for those unable to care for themselves, we believe in welfare reform that eliminates waste, fraud and abuse; requires work from those who are capable; limits time on public assistance; discourages illegitimacy; and reduces the burden on the taxpayers.

3

5. Because all Americans have the right to be safe in their homes, on their streets, and in their communities, we believe in tough law enforcement, especially against juvenile crime and the drug traffic, with stiff penalties, no loopholes, and judges who respect the rights of law-abiding Americans.

6. Because institutions like the family are the backbone of a healthy society, we believe government must support the rights of the family; and recognizing within our own ranks different approaches toward our common goal, we reaffirm respect for the sanctity of human life.

7. Because our children need and are entitled to the best education in the world, we believe in parental involvement and family choice in schooling, teacher authority and accountability, more control to local school boards, and emphasis upon the basics of learning in safe classrooms.

8. Because older Americans have built our past and direct us, in wisdom and experience, toward the future, we believe we must meet our nation's commitments to them by preserving and protecting Medicare and Social Security.

9. Because a good society rests on an ethical foundation, we believe families, communities, and religious institutions can best teach the American values of honesty, responsibility, hard work, compassion, and mutual respect.

10. Because our country's greatest strength is its people, not its government, we believe today's government is too large and intrusive and does too many things the people could do better for themselves.

11. Because we trust our fellow Americans, rather than centralized government, we believe the people, acting through their State and local elected officials, should have control over programs like education and welfare – thereby pushing power away from official Washington and returning it to the people in their communities and states.

12. Because we view the careful development of our country's natural resources as stewardship of creation, we believe property rights must be honored in our efforts to restore, protect, and enhance the environment for the generations to come.

13. Because we are all one America, we oppose discrimination. We believe in the equality of all people before the law and that individuals should be judged by their ability rather than their race, creed, or disability.

14. Because this is a difficult and dangerous world, we believe that peace can be assured only through strength, that a strong national defense is necessary to protect America at home and secure its interests abroad, and that we must restore leadership and character to the presidency as the best way to restore America's leadership and credibility throughout the world.

4

19 The Ten Biggest Donators to the Two National Parties

Founded in 1970 by John Gardner, a former secretary of the Department of Health, Education and Welfare, Common Cause is a nonpartisan, nonprofit public interest group with a membership of 250,000 citizens. Intended to make government more open and accountable, Common Cause traces the financial donations of elected officials nationwide, paying particular attention to the influence of "big money"— donations from wealthy organizations—on the American political process.

Published by Common Cause in its quarterly magazine, the first two tables list the largest U.S. corporations that have donated money to the Republican and Democratic parties, respectively, since January 1991. As demonstrated by the tables, the Republican party donors are more generous than their Democratic party counterparts. Moreover, the third table, Mixed Doubles, shows that these big donors, except for MCI, are more willing to give money to the Republican party than to the Democratic party when they make contributions to both of them.

The REPUBLICAN CLUB

These are the top 10 soft money donors to the Republican Party since January 1991. Their totals include contributions from executives and subsidiaries.

Amway Corp.	$ 2,810,000
Philip Morris Co. Inc.	$ 2,291,776
Archer Daniels Midland Co.	$ 1,682,268
RJR Nabisco	$ 1,626,757
American Financial Corp.	$ 1,475,000
Atlantic Richfield Co. (ARCO)	$ 1,336,113
Merrill Lynch & Co. Inc.	$ 925,700
U.S. Tobacco Co.	$ 865,466
Joseph E. Seagram & Sons Inc.	$ 724,727
Chevron Corp.	$ 708,422

The DEMOCRATIC CLUB

These are the top 10 soft money contributors to the Democratic Party since January 1991.
Where appropriate, executives and subsidiaries are included.

National Education Association	$ 1,132,913
American Federation of State, County and Municipal Employees	$ 996,944
Archer Daniels Midland Co. (ADM)	$ 819,000
Atlantic Richfield Co. (ARCO)	$ 732,648
Laborers' International Union of North America	$ 713,150
Joseph E. Seagram & Sons Inc.	$ 699,614
American Financial Corp.	$ 675,000
Connell Rice & Sugar Co.	$ 659,600
Service Employees International Union	$ 644,675
MCA Inc.	$ 634,003

MIXED DOUBLES

Here are the top 10 donors to both parties since January 1991.
Their contribution totals include donations from executives and company subsidiaries

	TO DEMOCRATS	TO REPUBLICANS	TOTAL
Philip Morris	$ 453,500	$ 2,291,776	$ 2,745,276
Archer Daniels Midland Co. (ADM)	$ 819,000	$ 1,682,268	$ 2,501,268
RJR Nabisco	$ 579,900	$ 1,626,757	$ 2,206,757
American Financial Corp.	$ 675,000	$ 1,475,000	$ 2,150,000
Atlantic Richfield Co. (ARCO)	$ 732,648	$ 1,336,113	$ 2,068,761
Joseph E. Seagram & Sons Inc.	$ 699,614	$ 724,727	$ 1,424,341
U.S. Tobacco Co.	$ 201,308	$ 865,466	$ 1,066,774
Merrill Lynch & Co. Inc.	$ 139,300	$ 925,700	$ 1,065,000
Chevron Corp.	$ 347,838	$ 708,422	$ 1,056,260
MCI Telecommunications Corp.	$ 569,214	$ 371,870	$ 941,084

9 ELECTIONS

20 A Sample Ballot from Broward County, Florida

Voting machines and ballots vary from state to state, so boards of elections create sample ballots to show voters how to cast their votes. On the next several pages is a sample ballot from Broward County, Florida, from the 1994 general election. As shown on the ballot, in addition to electing federal, state and local officials, Florida voters were given the opportunity to ratify or reject five state constitutional amendments in 1994. This procedure—to submit proposed laws directly to the voting public for ratification—is called a referendum. Referendums allow voters to get directly involved in the policy-making process.

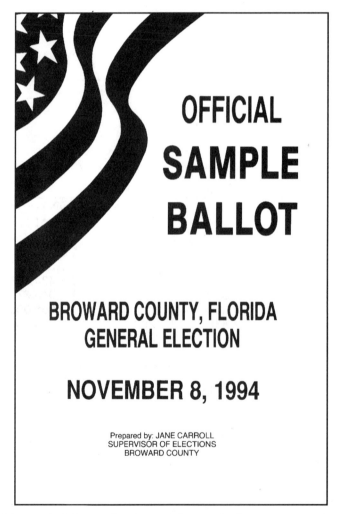

Courtesy of the Board of Elections from Broward County, Florida.

The information contained in this
Sample Ballot Booklet is available in
Spanish. If you need a copy, please
call 357-8452

La informacion en esta boleta puede
obtenerla en Espanol. Si necesita
una copia por favor llamar al 357-
8452.

BROWARD CITIZENS

October 1994

Dear Voter:

Due to the fact Broward County has sixty-nine different ballot styles because U.S. Congressmen, State Senators and State Representatives are in single member Districts and, therefore, do not run county-wide, we are sending you this sample ballot. This is the ballot as it will appear in your precinct. If you live in a city that has a special election on November 8, or Zone 1, 2 or 6 of the Central Broward Drainage District, you will be able to vote that also on the same voting unit; however, we are unable to include that information on the sample ballot.

It is our hope that by preparing this sample ballot for you, you will not find our different districts confusing. You will be able to study the ballot before you visit your polling place on November 8. You may also take this sample ballot to the precinct with you on election day if you would find it helpful.

The address of your polling place is printed on your blue voter identification card, which is helpful for identification at the polls on election day.

Broward County uses a Computer Election System. The use of this system will be explained to you as you enter the polling place.

Please call our office, 357-7050, if you have questions. At this time the phones are <u>very</u> busy. Please be patient.

Thank you and please vote.

Sincerely,

Jane Carroll
Supervisor of Elections

SUPERVISOR OF ELECTIONS

To vote for a write-in candidate, write title of
the office and the name of the candidate on
the grey envelope as shown above.

There are write-in candidates for several
offices as indicated on these ballot pages.

The pollworkers cannot give you the names
of the write-in candidates. Only officially
filed write-in candidates will have their votes
tabulated.

Voting Instructions

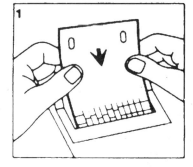

Step 1 Using both hands, insert the ballot card all the way into the Votomatic.

Step 2 Be sure the two slots in the end of your card fit down **over the two red pins.**

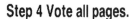

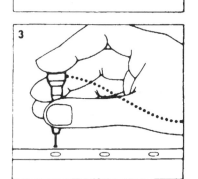

Step 3 To vote, use the punching instrument attached by chain to the Votomatic. **Punch straight down through** the hole to the right of the arrow by the candidate or issue of your choice. **Do not use any other punching instrument.**

Step 4 Vote all pages.

Step 5 After voting, remove the ballot card from the Votomatic, place it in the grey security envelope and take to the ballot box.

NOTE: If you make a mistake, return your ballot card and obtain another.

FOLLOWING ARE THE PAGES AS THEY WILL APPEAR IN YOUR PRECINCT.

1
D

OFFICIAL BALLOT, GENERAL ELECTION
BROWARD COUNTY, FLORIDA
NOVEMBER 8, 1994

CONGRESSIONAL			
UNITED STATES SENATOR (Vote for ONE)	HUGH E. RODHAM	DEMOCRAT	3 ➤
	CONNIE MACK	REPUBLICAN	4 ➤
	To vote for a write-in candidate, follow directions on the grey envelope.		

REPRESENTATIVE IN CONGRESS 20TH CONGRESSIONAL DISTRICT (Vote for ONE)	PETER DEUTSCH	DEMOCRAT	9 ➤
	BEVERLY "BEV" KENNEDY	REPUBLICAN	10 ➤

OFFICIAL BALLOT, GENERAL ELECTION
BROWARD COUNTY, FLORIDA
NOVEMBER 8, 1994

STATE

GOVERNOR AND LT. GOVERNOR (Vote for ONE)	**LAWTON CHILES** - For Governor **BUDDY MACKAY** - For Lt. Governor	DEMOCRAT	21 ▶
	JEB BUSH - For Governor **TOM FEENEY** - For Lt. Governor	REPUBLICAN	23 ▶
	To vote for a write-in candidate, follow directions on the grey envelope.		

SECRETARY OF STATE (Vote for ONE)	**RON SAUNDERS**	DEMOCRAT	27 ▶
	SANDY BARRINGER MORTHAM	REPUBLICAN	28 ▶

ATTORNEY GENERAL (Vote for ONE)	**BOB BUTTERWORTH**	DEMOCRAT	30 ▶
	HENRY FERRO	REPUBLICAN	31 ▶

COMPTROLLER (Vote for ONE)	**GERALD LEWIS**	DEMOCRAT	33 ▶
	BOB MILLIGAN	REPUBLICAN	34 ▶

TREASURER (Vote for ONE)	**BILL NELSON**	DEMOCRAT	36 ▶
	TIM IRELAND	REPUBLICAN	37 ▶
	To vote for a write-in candidate, follow directions on the grey envelope.		

OFFICIAL BALLOT, GENERAL ELECTION
BROWARD COUNTY, FLORIDA
NOVEMBER 8, 1994

STATE			
COMMISSIONER OF EDUCATION (Vote for ONE)	DOUG JAMERSON	DEMOCRAT	41 ▶▶
	FRANK T. BROGAN	REPUBLICAN	42 ▶▶

COMMISSIONER OF AGRICULTURE (Vote for ONE)	BOB CRAWFORD	DEMOCRAT	44 ▶▶
	JIM SMITH	REPUBLICAN	45 ▶▶

OFFICIAL BALLOT, GENERAL ELECTION
BROWARD COUNTY, FLORIDA
NOVEMBER 8, 1994

COUNTY

| COUNTY COMMISSIONER DISTRICT 4 (Vote for ONE) | SCOTT I. COWAN | DEMOCRAT | 60 ➤ |
| | WALTER T. SAMUELSON | REPUBLICAN | 61 ➤ |

| COUNTY COMMISSIONER DISTRICT 6 (Vote for ONE) | SUZANNE N. "SUE" GUNZBURGER | DEMOCRAT | 63 ➤ |
| | JAY D. FREDERICK | REPUBLICAN | 64 ➤ |

| COUNTY SCHOOL BOARD DISTRICT 1 (Vote for ONE) | ABRAHAM "ABE" FISCHLER | DEMOCRAT | 66 ➤ |
| | FERNANDO GUTIERREZ | REPUBLICAN | 67 ➤ |

| COUNTY SCHOOL BOARD DISTRICT 4 (Vote for ONE) | DONALD "DON" SAMUELS | DEMOCRAT | 69 ➤ |
| | LORNA BRYAN | REPUBLICAN | 70 ➤ |

SUPREME COURT

Shall Justice STEPHEN H. GRIMES of the Supreme Court be retained in office?	YES 73 ➤
	NO 74 ➤
Shall Justice GERALD KOGAN of the Supreme Court be retained in office?	YES 75 ➤
	NO 76 ➤

OFFICIAL BALLOT, GENERAL ELECTION
BROWARD COUNTY, FLORIDA
NOVEMBER 8, 1994

DISTRICT COURT OF APPEAL		
Shall Judge JOHN W. DELL of the Fourth District Court of Appeal be retained in office?	YES	79▶
	NO	80▶
Shall Judge BOBBY W. GUNTHER of the Fourth District Court of Appeal be retained in office?	YES	81▶
	NO	82▶
Shall Judge LARRY A. KLEIN of the Fourth District Court of Appeal be retained in office?	YES	83▶
	NO	84▶
Shall Judge BARBARA J. PARIENTE of the Fourth District Court of Appeal be retained in office?	YES	85▶
	NO	86▶
Shall Judge BARRY J. STONE of the Fourth District Court of Appeal be retained in office?	YES	87▶
	NO	88▶

COUNTY COURT JUDGE		
COUNTY COURT JUDGE GROUP 22 (Vote for ONE)	RONALD M. "RON" GUNZBURGER	92▶
	LISA GAIL TRACHMAN	93▶

OFFICIAL BALLOT, GENERAL ELECTION
BROWARD COUNTY, FLORIDA
NOVEMBER 8, 1994

STATE CONSTITUTIONAL AMENDMENTS

No. 1   **CONSTITUTIONAL AMENDMENT**
                               ARTICLE III, SECTION 3

**START OF REGULAR SESSIONS OF THE
LEGISLATURE**

Proposing an amendment to the State Constitution, effective upon approval, to provide that the annual 60-day regular sessions of the Legislature begin on the first Tuesday after the first Monday in March.

YES for Approval	120➤
NO for Rejection	121➤

No. 2   **CONSTITUTIONAL AMENDMENT**
                               ARTICLE VII, SECTION 1
                               ARTICLE XII, SECTION 21

LIMITATION ON STATE REVENUE COLLECTIONS

Limits state revenue collections to the prior year's allowed revenue plus an adjustment for growth based on the growth rate of state personal income over the preceding five years, with excess collections deposited in the budget stabilization fund until fully funded and then refunded to taxpayers. Defines "state revenues." Allows the Legislature to increase this limit by 2/3 vote. Requires adjustment of the limitation to reflect transfers of responsibility for funding governmental functions.

YES for Approval	126➤
NO for Rejection	127➤

No. 3   **CONSTITUTIONAL AMENDMENT**
                               ARTICLE X, SECTION 16

LIMITING MARINE NET FISHING

Limits the use of nets for catching saltwater finfish, shellfish, or other marine animals by prohibiting the use of gill and other entangling nets in all Florida waters, and prohibiting the use of other nets larger than 500 square feet in mesh area in nearshore and inshore Florida waters. Provides definitions, administrative and criminal penalties, and exceptions for scientific and governmental purposes.

YES for Approval	131➤
NO for Rejection	132➤

OFFICIAL BALLOT, GENERAL ELECTION
BROWARD COUNTY, FLORIDA
NOVEMBER 8, 1994

STATE CONSTITUTIONAL AMENDMENTS

No. 4

CONSTITUTIONAL AMENDMENT
ARTICLE XI, SECTION 3

REVENUE LIMITS: MAY PEOPLE'S AMENDMENTS LIMITING GOVERNMENT REVENUE BE ALLOWED TO COVER MULTIPLE SUBJECTS?

This provision would expand the people's rights to initiate constitutional changes limiting the power of government to raise revenue by allowing amendments to cover multiple subjects. This provision is effective immediately after voter approval for amendments effective thereafter.

YES for Approval	138▶
NO for Rejection	139▶

No. 8

CONSTITUTIONAL AMENDMENT
ARTICLE X, SECTION 7

LIMITED CASINOS

Authorizing a limited number of gaming casinos in Broward, Dade, Duval, Escambia, Hillsborough, Lee, Orange, Palm Beach and Pinellas Counties, with two in Miami Beach; and limited-size casinos with existing and operating pari-mutuel facilities; and if authorized by the legislature up to five limited-size riverboat casinos in the remaining counties, but only one per county. Mandating implementation by the legislature. Effective upon adoption, but prohibiting casino gaming until July 1, 1995.

YES for Approval	143▶
NO for Rejection	144▶

Only one booklet is being mailed to each household, regardless of how many are registered to vote, as an economy measure due to the high cost of postage. You may pick up additional copies as long as the supply lasts at the Broward County Governmental Center, Room 102, 115 S. Andrews Avenue, Fort Lauderdale.

NOTICE CONCERNING POLLING PLACE

Polling places are very difficult to get and to keep. The place where you vote is important in that voting is important; however, it cannot always be a place where you would choose to spend a significant amount of time. You will just spend a few minutes three or four times every other year.

We cannot change polling places easily. Some inconveniences may occur as they do in all phases of life. Please accept this.

If you know of a better place in your precinct, please do us a favor by checking on its availability and letting us know for future elections.

Thank you for your understanding.

Are you interested in helping out as a Pollworker?

The polls are staffed for November 8, 1994, but we are planning ahead for the '96 elections.

On election days in Broward County over 3,500 workers are stationed at our 597 polling locations to serve the voters. Efficiency and dedication are needed traits. Patience and friendliness are also essential.

Do you fill the bill? If so, we hope you will complete the application below and mail it to us as soon as possible. Once your application is processed, our office will contact you to attend an orientation session at our facility.

Thank you,

Jane Carroll
Supervisor of Elections

Pollworker Application
Please PRINT clearly and answer all questions.

Name _____
                Last   First   M.I.

Address _____
            Street   Apt #   City   Zip

Phone _____ Date of Birth _____

Voter Registration # _____ Social Security # _____

Precinct in which you are registered _____ Do you speak Spanish? _____

Do you have your own transportation? _____ Do you have a VCR? _____

Would you be willing to work in a precinct other than your own? _____

_____ _____
               Signature   Date

Detach the above Application and mail to:
Jane Carroll
Supervisor of Elections
Broward County Governmental Center
115 S. Andrews Ave., Room 102
Fort Lauderdale, FL 33301
Phone: 357-7050

The National Voter Registration Act of 1993 (also known as the Motor Voter Bill) is considered to have simplified and liberalized U.S. voter registration laws. The law requires states to provide voter registration forms at motor vehicle offices as well as at military recruiting stations and welfare offices. The law also allows citizens to register to vote through the mail. Seven states have filed legal actions against the law, arguing that it infringes on states' rights, but it has been upheld by various federal courts. The implementation of the law during the 1996 primary election season neither expanded voter participation as dramatically as its proponents had advocated, nor did it spawn significant election fraud as its opponents had warned. Here is a brief excerpt from that law.

PUBLIC LAW 103-31—MAY 20, 1993   107 STAT. 77

Public Law 103–31
103d Congress

An Act

To establish national voter registration procedures for Federal elections, and for other purposes.

Be it enacted by the Senate and House of Representatives of the United States of America in Congress assembled,

SECTION 1. SHORT TITLE.

This Act may be cited as the "National Voter Registration Act of 1993".

SEC. 2. FINDINGS AND PURPOSES.

(a) FINDINGS.—The Congress finds that—
(1) the right of citizens of the United States to vote is a fundamental right;
(2) it is the duty of the Federal, State, and local governments to promote the exercise of that right; and
(3) discriminatory and unfair registration laws and procedures can have a direct and damaging effect on voter participation in elections for Federal office and disproportionately harm voter participation by various groups, including racial minorities.
(b) PURPOSES.—The purposes of this Act are—
(1) to establish procedures that will increase the number of eligible citizens who register to vote in elections for Federal office;
(2) to make it possible for Federal, State, and local governments to implement this Act in a manner that enhances the participation of eligible citizens as voters in elections for Federal office;
(3) to protect the integrity of the electoral process; and
(4) to ensure that accurate and current voter registration rolls are maintained.

SEC. 3. DEFINITIONS.

As used in this Act—
(1) the term "election" has the meaning stated in section 301(1) of the Federal Election Campaign Act of 1971 (2 U.S.C. 431(1));
(2) the term "Federal office" has the meaning stated in section 301(3) of the Federal Election Campaign Act of 1971 (2 U.S.C. 431(3));
(3) the term "motor vehicle driver's license" includes any personal identification document issued by a State motor vehicle authority;

Margin notes:
May 20, 1993
[H.R. 2]

National Voter Registration Act of 1993.
Intergovernmental relations.
42 USC 1973gg note.
42 USC 1973gg.

42 USC 1973gg-1.

Document of the U.S. House of Representatives.

10 CONGRESS

22 Excerpts from a House of Representatives Calendar

A congressional calendar is an agenda for the legislature on which pending business items are listed. The U.S. Senate uses two types of calendars: a *calendar of business* for legislative matters and an *executive calendar* for executive affairs. In contrast, the House of Representatives uses several legislative calendars; including a *union calendar*, a *House calendar*, a *private calendar*, a *corrections calendar*, and a *discharge calendar*. Pages of each are shown here. The entire calendar for the House of Representatives is almost two hundred pages long.

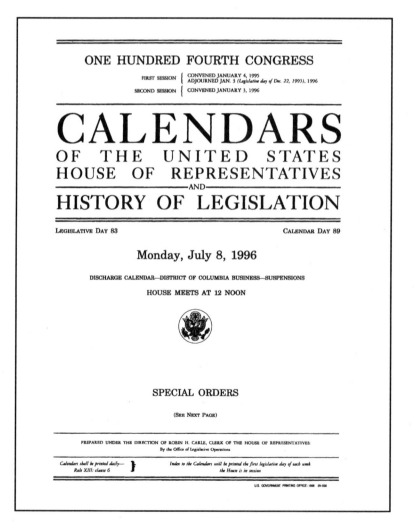

Document of the House of Representatives.

SPECIAL ORDERS

HOUR OF MEETING

On motion of Mr. Watts of Oklahoma, by unanimous consent, *Ordered,* That when the House adjourns Monday, July 8, 1996, it adjourn to meet at 12:30 p.m. on Tuesday, July 9, 1996. (Agreed to June 28, 1996.)

HOUR OF MEETING

On motion of Mr. Watts of Oklahoma, by unanimous consent, *Ordered,* That when the House adjourns Tuesday, July 9, 1996, it adjourn to meet at 9 a.m. on Wednesday, July 10, 1996. (Agreed to June 28, 1996.)

RECESS

On motion of Mr. Watts of Oklahoma, by unanimous consent, *Ordered,* That on Wednesday, July 10, 1996 that it shall be in order to declare a recess at any time subject to the call of the Chair for the purpose of receiving in Joint Meeting His Excellency Binyamin Netanyahu, Prime Minister of Israel. (Agreed to June 28, 1996.)

CALENDAR WEDNESDAY BUSINESS

On motion of Mr. Watts of Oklahoma, by unanimous consent, *Ordered,* That business in order under the Calendar Wednesday rule be dispensed with on Wednesday, July 10, 1996. (Agreed to June 28, 1996.)

SPECIAL ORDER SPEECHES

The format for recognition for morning hour debate and restricted special order speeches, which began on February 23, 1994, will continue until the adjournment of the 2nd Session of the 104th Congress sine die as outlined below:

On Tuesday, following legislative business, the Chair may recognize Members for special order speeches up to midnight, and such speeches may not extend beyond midnight. On all other days of the week, the Chair may recognize Members for special order speeches up to 4 hours after the conclusion of 5-minute special order speeches. Such speeches may not extend beyond the 4-hour limit without the permission of the Chair, which may grant it only with advance consultation between the leaderships and notification to the House. However, at no time shall the Chair recognize for any special order speeches beyond midnight.

The Chair will first recognize Members for 5-minute special order speeches, alternating initially and subsequentially between the parties, regardless of the date the order was granted by the House. The Chair will then recognize longer special order speeches. The 4-hour limitation will be divided between the majority and minority parties. Each party is entitled to reserve its first hour for respective leaderships or their designees. Recognition will alternate initially and subsequentially between the parties, regardless of the date the order was granted by the House.

The allocation of time within each party's 2-hour period, or shorter period if prorated to end by midnight, is to be determined by a list submitted to the Chair by the respective leaderships. Members may not sign up for any special order earlier than 1 week prior to the special order, and additional guidelines may be established for such signups by the respective leaderships.

MORNING HOUR DEBATE

On motion of Mr. Armey, by unanimous consent, *Ordered,* That until the adjournment of the 2nd Session of the 104th Congress Sine Die the House shall convene 90 minutes earlier than the time otherwise established by order of the House on Mondays and Tuesdays of each week solely for the purpose of conducting "morning hour" debates under the following conditions: 1. The Prayer by the Chaplain, approval of the Journal, and the pledge of allegiance to the flag shall be postponed until resumption of the House session following the completion of morning hour debate; 2. Debate shall be limited to thirty minutes allocated to each party, with initial and subsequent recognitions alternating between parties; 3. Recognition shall be conferred by the Speaker pursuant to lists submitted by the respective leaderships; 4. No Member shall be permitted to address the House for longer than five minutes except for the Majority Leader, Minority Leader, and Minority Whip; and 5. Morning hour debate shall be followed by a recess declared by the Speaker pursuant to clause 12 of rule 1, until the appointed hour for the resumption of legislative business.

Provided, further that on Tuesdays falling after May 14 of each year -

the House shall convene for such debates one hour earlier than the time otherwise established by order of the House (rather than 90 minutes earlier); and

the time for such debates shall be limited to 25 minutes allocated to each Party (rather than 30 minutes to each); but

in no event shall such debates continue beyond the time that falls 10 minutes before the appointed hour for the resumption of legislative business.

TABLE OF CONTENTS

SEC. 1

SEC. 2

SEC. 3

SEC. 4

SEC. 5

SEC. 6

SEC. 7

SEC. 8

SEC. 9

SEC. 10

SEC. 11

SEC. 12

SEC. 13

SEC. 14

SEC. 15

SEC. 16

SEC. 17

SEC. 18

SEC. 19

SEC. 20

THE MORNING HOUR FOR THE CALL OF COMMITTEES

Rule XXIV, clause 4:

"4. After the unfinished business has been disposed of, the Speaker shall call each standing committee in regular order, and then select committees, and each committee when named may call up for consideration any bill reported by it on a previous day and on the House Calendar, and if the Speaker shall not complete the call of the Committees before the House passes to other business, he shall resume the next call where he left off, giving preference to the last bill under consideration: *Provided*, That whenever any committee shall have occupied the morning hour on two days, it shall not be in order to call up any other bill until the other committees have been called in their turn."

NOTE.—Call rests with the Committee on Agriculture.

CALENDAR WEDNESDAY BUSINESS

Rule XXIV, clause 7:

"7. On Wednesday of each week no business shall be in order except as provided by clause 4 of this rule unless the House by a two-thirds vote on motion to dispense therewith shall otherwise determine. On such a motion there may be debate not to exceed five minutes for and against. On a call of committees under this rule bills may be called up from either the House or the Union Calendar, excepting bills which are privileged under the rules; but bills called up from the Union Calendar shall be considered in the Committee of the Whole House on the state of the Union. This rule shall not apply during the last two weeks of the session. It shall not be in order for the Speaker to entertain a motion for a recess on any Wednesday except during the last two weeks of the session: *Provided*, That not more than two hours of general debate shall be permitted on any measure called up on Calendar Wednesday, and all debate must be confined to the subject matter of the bill, the time to be equally divided between those for and against the bill: *Provided further*, That whenever any committee shall have occupied one Wednesday it shall not be in order, unless the House by a two-thirds vote shall otherwise determine, to consider any unfinished business previously called up by such committee, unless the previous question had been ordered thereon, upon any succeeding Wednesday until the other committees have been called in their turn under this rule: *Provided*, That when, during any one session of a Congress, all of the committees of the House are not called under the Calendar Wednesday rule, at the next session of that Congress the call shall commence where it left off at the end of the preceding session."

NOTE.—Call rests with the Committee on Agriculture.

SPECIAL LEGISLATIVE DAYS

Calendar Wednesday	Wednesday of each week, except during the last 2 weeks of a session (clause 7, rule XXIV).
Corrections Calendar	Second and fourth Tuesdays of each month (clause 4, rule XIII).
Discharge Calendar	Second and fourth Mondays of each month, except during the last 6 days of a session (clause 3, rule XXVII).
District of Columbia business	Second and fourth Mondays of each month (clause 8, rule XXIV).
Private Calendar	First and third Tuesdays of each month (clause 6, rule XXIV).
Suspension of rules	Mondays and Tuesdays and during the last 6 days of a session (clause 1, rule XXVII).

1. UNION CALENDAR

Rule XIII, clause 1 (First):
"First. A Calendar of the Committee of the Whole House on the state of the Union, to which shall be referred bills raising revenue, general appropriation bills, and bills of a public character directly or indirectly appropriating money or property."

1995			No.
Jan. 24	Referred to the Committee of the Whole House on the State of the Union. (H. Doc. 104–1)	Message of the President of the United States to the Congress on the subject of the state of the Union.	1
H.R. 845 Feb. 10	Mr. Livingston (Appropriations). Rept. 104–30	Rescinding certain budget authority, and for other purposes.	13
H.R. 1159 Mar. 8	Mr. Livingston (Appropriations). Rept. 104–71	Making supplemental appropriations and rescissions for the fiscal year ending September 30, 1995, and for other purposes.	37
H.R. 1135 Mar. 14	Mr. Roberts (Agriculture). Rept. 104–77	To improve the Commodity Distribution Programs of the Department of Agriculture, to reform and simplify the Food Stamp Program, and for other purposes.	39
H.R. 1216 Mar. 23	Mr. Bliley (Commerce). Rept. 104–86	To amend the Atomic Energy Act of 1954 to provide for the privatization of the United States Enrichment Corporation.	41
H.R. 1218 Mar. 23	Mr. Bliley (Commerce). Rept. 104–88	To extend the authority of the Federal Communications Commission to use competitive bidding in granting licenses and permits.	42
H.R. 618 Apr. 6	Mr. Roberts (Agriculture). Rept. 104–104	To extend the authorization for appropriations for the Commodity Futures Trading Commission through fiscal year 2000.	48
H.R. 1323 May 1 Part I	Mr. Shuster (Transportation and Infrastructure).	To reduce risk to public safety and the environment associated with pipeline transportation of natural gas and hazardous liquids, and for other purposes.	58
June 1 Part II	Mr. Bliley (Commerce). Rept. 104–110		

(1–1)

2. HOUSE CALENDAR

> Rule XIII, clause 1 (Second):
> "Second. A House Calendar, to which shall be referred all bills of a public character not raising revenue nor directly or indirectly appropriating money or property."

			No.
1995 H.J. Res. 2 Mar. 6	Mr. Canady (Judiciary). Rept. 104–67	Proposing an amendment to the Constitution of the United States with respect to the number of terms of office of Members of the Senate and the House of Representatives.	**27**
Rept. 104–401 Dec. 12	Mrs. Johnson of Connecticut (Standards of Official Conduct).	Inquiry into Various Complaints Filed Against Representative Newt Gingrich.	**148**
1996 H.R. 2297 May 14	Mr. Hyde (Judiciary). Rept. 104–573	To codify without substantive change laws related to transportation and to improve the United States Code.	**222**
H. Res. 438 May 16	Mr. Diaz-Balart (Rules). Rept. 104–582	Providing for consideration of the bill (H.R. 3144) to establish a United States policy for the deployment of a national missile defense system, and for other purposes.	**226**
H.R. 3134 May 21	Mr. Shuster (Transportation and Infrastructure). Rept. 104–587	To designate the United States Courthouse under construction at 1030 Southwest 3rd Avenue, Portland, Oregon, as the "Mark O. Hatfield United States Courthouse", and for other purposes.	**227**
Rept. 104–598 May 29	Mr. Clinger (Government Reform and Oversight).	Proceedings Against John M. Quinn, David Watkins, and Matthew Moore.	**231**
H.R. 3387 May 14 Resources discharged	To designate the Southern Piedmont Conservation Research Center located at 1420 Experimental Station Road in Watkinsville, Georgia, as the "J. Phil Campbell, Senior Natural Resource Conservation Center".	249	
June 27	Mr. Roberts (Agriculture). Rept. 104–645		

3. PRIVATE CALENDAR

Rule XIII, clause 1 (Third):

"Third. A Calendar of the Committee of the Whole House, to which shall be referred all bills of a private character."

Rule XXIV, clause 6:

"6. On the first Tuesday of each month after disposal of such business on the Speaker's table as requires reference only, the Speaker shall direct the Clerk to call the bills and resolutions on the Private Calendar. Should objection be made by two or more Members to the consideration of any bill or resolution so called, it shall be recommitted to the committee which reported the bill or resolution, and no reservation of objection shall be entertained by the Speaker. Such bills and resolutions, if considered, shall be considered in the House as in the Committee of the Whole. No other business shall be in order on this day unless the House, by two-thirds vote on motion to dispense therewith, shall otherwise determine. On such motion debate shall be limited to five minutes for and five minutes against said motion.

"On the third Tuesday of each month after the disposal of such business on the Speaker's table as requires reference only, the Speaker may direct the Clerk to call the bills and resolutions on the Private Calendar, preference to be given to omnibus bills containing bills or resolutions which have previously been objected to on a call of the Private Calendar. All bills and resolutions on the Private Calendar so called, if considered, shall be considered in the House as in the Committee of the Whole. Should objection be made by two or more Members to the consideration of any bill or resolution other than an omnibus bill, it shall be recommitted to the committee which reported the bill or resolution and no reservation of objection shall be entertained by the Speaker.

"Omnibus bills shall be read for amendment by paragraph, and no amendment shall be in order except to strike out or to reduce amounts of money stated or to provide limitations. Any item or matter stricken from an omnibus bill shall not thereafter during the same session of Congress be included in any omnibus bill.

"Upon passage of any such omnibus bill, said bill shall be resolved into the several bills and resolutions of which it is composed, and such original bills and resolutions, with any amendments adopted by the House, shall be engrossed, where necessary, and proceedings thereon had as if said bills and resolutions had been passed in the House severally.

"In the consideration of any omnibus bill the proceedings as set forth above shall have the same force and effect as if each Senate and House bill or resolution therein contained or referred to were considered by the House as a separate and distinct bill or resolution."

1996			No.
H.R. 2001	Mr. Hyde (Judiciary).	For the relief of Norton R. Girault.	6
June 26	Rept. 104–637		
S. 966	Mr. Hyde (Judiciary).	For the relief of Nathan C. Vance, and for other purposes.	7
June 26	Rept. 104–638		

4. CORRECTIONS CALENDAR

Rule XIII, clause 4:

"4. (a) After a bill has been favorably reported and placed on either the Union or House Calendar, the Speaker may, after consultation with the Minority Leader, file with the Clerk a notice requesting that such bill also be placed upon a special calendar to be known as the 'Corrections Calendar.' On the second and fourth Tuesdays of each month, after the Pledge of Allegiance, the Speaker may direct the Clerk to call the bills in numerical order which have been on the Corrections Calendar for three legislative days.

"(b) A bill so called shall be considered in the House, shall be debatable for one hour equally divided and controlled by the chairman and ranking minority member of the primary committee of jurisdiction reporting the bill, and shall not be subject to amendment except those amendments recommended by the primary committee of jurisdiction or those offered by the chairman of the primary committee or a designee. The previous question shall be considered as ordered on the bill and any amendment thereto to final passage without intervening motion except one motion to recommit with or without instructions.

"(c) A three-fifths vote of the Members voting shall be required to pass any bill called from the Corrections Calendar but the rejection of any such bill, or the sustaining of any point of order against it or its consideration, shall not cause it to be removed from the Calendar to which it was originally referred."

1996 H.R. 2779 June 26	Mr. Walker (Science). Rept. 104–639 (Union Calendar 319)	To provide for soft-metric conversion, and for other purposes.	No. **19**

(4–1)

CALENDAR OF MOTIONS TO DISCHARGE COMMITTEES

Rule XXVII, clause 3:

"3. A Member may present to the Clerk a motion in writing to discharge a committee from the consideration of a public bill or resolution which has been referred to it thirty days prior thereto (but only one motion may be presented for each bill or resolution). Under this rule it shall also be in order for a Member to file a motion to discharge the Committee on Rules from further consideration of any resolution providing either a special order of business, or a special rule for the consideration of any public bill or resolution favorably reported by a standing committee, or a special rule for the consideration of a public bill or resolution which has remained in a standing committee thirty or more days without action: *Provided*, That said resolution from which it is moved to discharge the Committee on Rules has been referred to that committee at least seven days prior to the filing of the motion to discharge. The motion shall be placed in the custody of the Clerk, who shall arrange some convenient place for the signature of Members. A signature may be withdrawn by a Member in writing at any time before the motion is entered on the Journal. Once a motion to discharge has been filed, the Clerk shall make the signatures a matter of public record. The Clerk shall cause the names of the Members who have signed a discharge motion during any week to be published in a portion of the Congressional Record designated for that purpose on the last legislative day of that week. The Clerk shall make available each day for public inspection in an appropriate office of the House cumulative lists of such names. The Clerk shall devise a means by which to make such lists available to offices of the House and to the public in electronic form. When a majority of the total membership of the House shall have signed the motion, it shall be entered on the Journal, printed with the signatures thereto in the Congressional Record, and referred to the Calendar of Motions to Discharge Committees.

"On the second and fourth Mondays of each month except during the last six days of any session of Congress, immediately after the approval of the Journal, any Member who has signed a motion to discharge which has been on the calendar at least seven days prior thereto, and seeks recognition, shall be recognized for the purpose of calling up the motion, and the House shall proceed to its consideration in the manner herein provided without intervening motion except one motion to adjourn. Recognition for the motions shall be in the order in which they have been entered on the Journal.

"When any motion under this rule shall be called up, the bill or resolution shall be read by title only. After twenty minutes' debate, one-half in favor of the proposition and one-half in opposition thereto, the House shall proceed to vote on the motion to discharge. If the motion prevails to discharge the Committee on Rules from any resolution pending before the committee, the House shall immediately consider such resolution, the Speaker not entertaining any dilatory motion except one motion to adjourn, and, if such resolution is adopted, the House shall immediately proceed to its execution. If the motion prevails to discharge one of the standing committees of the House from any public bill or resolution pending before the committee, it shall then be in order for any Member who signed the motion to move that the House proceed to the immediate consideration of such bill or resolution (such motion not being debatable), and such motion is hereby made of high privilege; and if it shall be decided in the affirmative, the bill shall be immediately considered under the general rules of the House, and if unfinished before adjournment of the day on which it is called up it shall remain the unfinished business until it is fully disposed of. Should the House by vote decide against the immediate consideration of such bill or resolution, it shall be referred to its proper calendar and be entitled to the same rights and privileges that it would have had had the committee to which it was referred duly reported same to the House for its consideration: *Provided,* That when any perfected motion to discharge a committee from the consideration of any public bill or resolution has once been acted upon by the House it shall not be in order to entertain during the same session of Congress any other motion for the discharge from that committee of said measure, or from any other committee of any other bill or resolution substantially the same, relating in substance to or dealing with the same subject matter, or from the Committee on Rules of a resolution providing a special order of business for the consideration of any other such bill or resolution, in order that such action by the House on a motion to discharge shall be res adjudicata for the remainder of that session: *Provided further,* That if before any one motion to discharge a committee has been acted upon by the House there are on the Calendar of Motions to Discharge Committees other motions to discharge committees from the consideration of bills or resolutions substantially the same, relating in substance to or dealing with the same subject matter, after the House shall have acted on one motion to discharge, the remaining said motions shall be stricken from the Calendar of Motions to Discharge Committees and not acted on during the remainder of that session of Congress."

Motion No. and date entered	Title	Committee	Motion filed by—	Cal-endar No.
1996				

(5–1)

HISTORY OF BILLS AND RESOLUTIONS

Numerical order of bills and resolutions which have been reported to or considered by either or both Houses.

NOTE. Similar or identical bills, and bills having reference to each other, are indicated by number in parentheses.

No.	Index Key and History of Bill	No.	Index Key and History of Bill

HOUSE BILLS

H.R. 1 (H. Res. 6) (S. 2).—To make certain laws applicable to the legislative branch of the Federal Government. Referred to Economic and Educational Opportunities and in addition to House Oversight, Government Reform and Oversight, Rules, and the Judiciary Jan. 4, 1995. Passed House Jan. 5 (Legislative day of Jan. 4), 1995; Roll No. 15: 429–0. Received in Senate Jan. 9, 1995. Ordered placed on the calendar Jan. 11 (Legislative day of Jan. 10), 1995. Passed Senate with amendment Jan. 12 (Legislative day of Jan. 10), 1995. See S. 2 for further action.

H.R. 2 (H. Res. 55) (S. 4).—To give the President item veto authority over appropriation Acts and targeted tax benefits in revenue Acts. Referred to Government Reform and Oversight and in addition to Rules Jan. 4, 1995. Reported amended from Rules Jan. 27, 1995; Rept. 104–11, Pt. I. Reported amended from Government Reform and Oversight Jan. 30, 1995; Pt. II. Union Calendar. Considered Feb. 2, 3, 1995. Passed House amended Feb. 6, 1995; Roll No. 95: 294–134. Received in Senate and referred jointly to the Budget and Governmental Affairs Feb. 7 (Legislative day of Jan. 30), 1995.

H.R. 4 (H. Res. 117) (H. Res. 119) (H.R. 1214) (H.R. 1135) (H. Res. 319).—To restore the American family, reduce illegitimacy, control welfare spending and reduce welfare dependence. Referred severally to Ways and Means, Banking and Financial Services, Economic and Educational Opportunities, the Budget, Rules, Commerce, the Judiciary, and Agriculture Jan. 4, 1995. Considered Mar. 21, 22, 23, 1995. Passed House amended Mar. 24, 1995; Roll No. 269: 234–199. Received in Senate and referred to Finance Mar. 29 (Legislative day of Mar. 27), 1995. Reported with amendments June 9 (Legislative day of June 5), 1995; Rept. 104–96. Considered Aug. 5, 7, 8, 11 (Legislative day of July 10), Sept. 6, 7, 8, 11, 12, 13, 14, 15 (Legislative day of Sept. 5), 1995. Passed Senate with amendments Sept. 19 (Legislative day of Sept. 5), 1995; Roll No. 443: 87–12. Senate insisted on its amendments and asked for a conference Sept. 19 (Legislative day of Sept. 5), 1995. House disagreed to Senate amendments and agreed to a conference Sept. 29, 1995. Conference report filed in the House Dec. 20, 1995; Rept. 104–430. House agreed to conference report Dec. 21, 1995; Roll No. 877: 245–178. Conference report considered in Senate Dec. 21, 1995. Senate agreed to conference report Dec. 22, 1995; Roll No. 613: 52–47. Presented to the President Dec. 29, 1995. Vetoed Jan. 9, 1996. In House, veto referred to Ways and Means Jan. 22, 1996.

HOUSE BILLS—Continued

H.R. 5 (H. Res. 38) (S. 1) (S. 169).—To curb the practice of imposing unfunded Federal mandates on States and local governments, to ensure that the Federal Government pays the costs incurred by those governments in complying with certain requirements under Federal statutes and regulations, and to provide information on the cost of Federal mandates on the private sector, and for other purposes. Referred to Government Reform and Oversight and in addition to Rules, the Budget, and the Judiciary Jan. 4, 1995. Reported amended from Rules Jan. 13, 1995; Rept. 104–1, Pt. I. Reported amended from Government Reform and Oversight Jan. 13, 1995; Pt. II. Considered Jan. 19, 20, 23, 24, 27, 30, 31, 1995. Passed House amended Feb. 1, 1995; Roll No. 83: 360–74. See S. 1 for further action.

H.R. 7 (H. Res. 83).—To revitalize the national security of the United States. Referred severally to International Relations, National Security, Intelligence, and the Budget Jan. 4, 1995. Reported amended from National Security Feb. 6, 1995; Rept. 104–18, Pt. I. Reported amended from International Relations Feb. 6, 1995; Pt. II. Reported amended from Intelligence Feb. 6, 1995; Pt. III. Considered Feb. 15, 1995. Passed House amended Feb. 16, 1995; Roll No. 145: 241–181. Received in Senate and referred to Foreign Relations Feb. 22, 1995.

H.R. 9 (H.R. 830) (H.R. 925) (H.R. 926) (H.R. 1022).— To create jobs, enhance wages, strengthen property rights, maintain certain economic liberties, decentralize and reduce the power of the Federal Government with respect to the States, localities, and citizens of the United States, and to increase the accountability of Federal officials. Referred severally to Ways and Means, Commerce, Government Reform and Oversight, the Budget, Rules, the Judiciary, and Science Jan. 4, 1995. Rereferred to Small Business Feb. 9, 1995. Reported amended from Commerce Feb. 15, 1995; Rept. 104–33, Pt. I. Reported amended from Science Feb. 15, 1995; Pt. II. Passed House amended Mar. 3, 1995; Roll No. 199: 277–141. Received in Senate and referred to Governmental Affairs Mar. 9 (Legislative day of Mar. 6), 1995.

H.R. 10.—To reform the Federal civil justice system; to reform product liability law. Referred severally to Commerce, the Judiciary, and Rules Jan. 4, 1995. Reported amended from Commerce Feb. 24, 1995; Rept. 104–50, Pt. I.

A Senate executive calendar for a particular day lists all pending nonlegislative matters awaiting action by the U.S. Senate. It encompasses all treaties to be ratified as well as all presidential nominations to be confirmed. Items are listed chronologically, according to the dates they are reported to the Senate by the appropriate committee of jurisdiction.

SENATE OF THE UNITED STATES
ONE HUNDRED FOURTH CONGRESS

FIRST SESSION { CONVENED JANUARY 4, 1995
ADJOURNED JANUARY 3, 1996

SECOND SESSION { CONVENED JANUARY 3, 1996

EXECUTIVE CALENDAR

Thursday, January 25, 1996

PREPARED UNDER THE DIRECTION OF KELLY D. JOHNSTON,
SECRETARY OF THE SENATE

By David G. Marcos, Executive Clerk

Document of the U.S. Senate.

Unanimous Consent Agreement

Ordered, That if the Chemical Weapons Convention (Tr. Doc. 103-21) has not been reported by the close of business on April 30, 1996, that the Convention be discharged from the Foreign Relations Committee and placed on the Executive Calendar.

(December 7, 1995)

Ordered, That when the Senate resumes executive session to consider the resolution of ratification to the START II TREATY, there be six hours for debate, to be equally divided in the usual form, with unlimited additional time under the control of the Senator from South Carolina (Mr. Thurmond), and that following the conclusion or yielding back of time, the Senate proceed to vote on adoption of the resolution of ratification, without further action or debate.

(December 22, 1995)

1
RESOLUTIONS

CALENDAR No.	EX. RES No.	SUBJECT	REPORTED BY

82

2

TREATIES

Calendar No.	Treaty Doc. No.	Subject	Reported By
11	103-1	TREATY WITH THE RUSSIAN FEDERATION ON FURTHER REDUCTION AND LIMITATION OF STRATEGIC OFFENSIVE ARMS (THE START II TREATY) .	Dec 15 95 Reported favorably by Mr. Helms, Committee on Foreign Relations, with a resolution of advice and consent to ratification, subject to six conditions and seven declarations. Printed report (Ex. Rept. 104-10).

3
NOMINATIONS

CALENDAR No.	MESSAGE No.	NOMINEE, OFFICE, AND PREDECESSOR	REPORTED By
		METROPOLITAN WASHINGTON AIRPORTS AUTHORITY	
* 251	7	Robert Clarke Brown, of New York, to be a Member of the Board of Directors of the Metropolitan Washington Airports Authority for a term of six years, vice Jack Edwards, term expired.	Jul 20, 95 Reported by Mr. Pressler, Committee on Commerce, Science, and Transportation, without printed report.
		NATIONAL FOUNDATION ON THE ARTS AND THE HUMANITIES	
* 258	355	Richard J. Stern, of Illinois, to be a Member of the National Council on the Arts for a term expiring September 3, 2000, vice Catherine Yi-yu Cho Woo, term expired.	Jul 24, 95 Reported by Mrs. Kassebaum, Committee on Labor and Human Resources, without printed report.
		UNITED STATES INSTITUTE OF PEACE	
* 324	258	Daniel A. Mica, of Virginia, to be a Member of the Board of Directors of the United States Institute of Peace for a term expiring January 19, 1997, vice W. Scott Thompson, term expired.	Sep 26, 95 Reported by Mrs. Kassebaum, Committee on Labor and Human Resources, without printed report.
		DEPARTMENT OF ENERGY	
* 330	466	Derrick L. Forrister, of Tennessee, to be an Assistant Secretary of Energy (Congressional and Intergovernmental Affairs), vice William J. Taylor, III, resigned.	Oct 11, 95 Reported by Mr. Murkowski, Committee on Energy and Natural Resources, without printed report.
		EXECUTIVE OFFICE OF THE PRESIDENT	
* 346	537	Alicia Haydock Munnell, of Massachusetts, to be a Member of the Council of Economic Advisers, vice Laura D'Andrea Tyson.	Oct 26, 95 Reported by Mr. D'Amato, Committee on Banking, Housing, and Urban Affairs, without printed report.
		SECURITIES AND EXCHANGE COMMISSION	
* 347	571	Isaac C. Hunt, Jr., of Ohio, to be a Member of the Securities and Exchange Commission for the term expiring June 5, 2000, vice Richard Y. Roberts, resigned.	Oct 26, 95 Reported by Mr. D'Amato, Committee on Banking, Housing, and Urban Affairs, without printed report.

* Signifies nominee's commitment to respond to requests to appear and testify before any duly constituted committee of the Senate

CALENDAR No.	MESSAGE No.	NOMINEE, OFFICE, AND PREDECESSOR	REPORTED BY
		NAVY	
365	275	The following named captain in the line of the United States Navy for promotion to the permanent grade of rear admiral (lower half), pursuant to Title 10, United States Code, Section 624, subject to qualifications, therefore, as provided by law: **Unrestricted Line Officer** *to be Rear Admiral (Lower Half)* Capt. John B. Padgett, III, 049-38-6225, U.S. Navy	Oct 31, 95 Reported by Mr. Thurmond, Committee on Armed Services, without printed report.
		DEPARTMENT OF TRANSPORTATION	
* 384	636	Charles A. Hunnicutt, of Georgia, to be an Assistant Secretary of Transportation, vice Jeffrey Neil Shane, resigned.	Nov 9, 95 Reported by Mr. Pressler, Committee on Commerce, Science, and Transportation, without printed report.
		DEPARTMENT OF DEFENSE	
* 397	695	Arthur L. Money, of California, to be an Assistant Secretary of the Air Force, vice Clark G. Fiester.	Nov 29, 95 Reported by Mr. Thurmond, Committee on Armed Services, without printed report.
		THE JUDICIARY	
434	615	Merrick B. Garland, of Maryland, to be United States Circuit Judge for the District of Columbia Circuit, vice Abner J. Mikva, retired.	Dec 14, 95 Reported by Mr. Hatch, Committee on the Judiciary, without printed report.
		DEPARTMENT OF STATE	
* 449	795	Rita Derrick Hayes, of Maryland, for the rank of Ambassador during her tenure of service as Chief Textile Negotiator.	Dec 22, 95 Reported by Mr. Helms, Committee on Foreign Relations, without printed report.

Signifies nominee's commitment to respond to requests to appear and testify before any duly constituted committee of the Senate

Many members of the 104th Congress tried to reach a balanced budget agreement. The Line Item Veto Act of 1996 may be the sole success of these efforts. By allowing the president to veto specific items in spending bills, the Act shifts some of the power of the purse from Congress to the president. Some critics think this Act is unconstitutional, claiming that it alters the system of checks and balances. Moreover, the Judicial Conference of the United States, which represents the federal judges, publicly denounced the measure prior to the congressional vote. The Judiciary Conference argued that this measure would pose a threat to the independence of the judicial branch because it would allow the president to retaliate against judges by vetoing items in judicial appropriations bills. Shown here are the first two pages of the thirteen-page law.

---

110 STAT. 1200   PUBLIC LAW 104–130—APR. 9, 1996

Public Law 104–130
104th Congress

An Act

Apr. 9, 1996
[S. 4]

To give the President line item veto authority with respect to appropriations, new direct spending, and limited tax benefits.

Line Item Veto Act.
2 USC 681 note.

Be it enacted by the Senate and House of Representatives of the United States of America in Congress assembled,

SECTION 1. SHORT TITLE.

This Act may be cited as the "Line Item Veto Act".

SEC. 2. LINE ITEM VETO AUTHORITY.

(a) IN GENERAL.—Title X of the Congressional Budget and Impoundment Control Act of 1974 (2 U.S.C. 681 et seq.) is amended by adding at the end the following new part:

"PART C—LINE ITEM VETO

"LINE ITEM VETO AUTHORITY

2 USC 691.

"SEC. 1021. (a) IN GENERAL.—Notwithstanding the provisions of parts A and B, and subject to the provisions of this part, the President may, with respect to any bill or joint resolution that has been signed into law pursuant to Article I, section 7, of the Constitution of the United States, cancel in whole—
  "(1) any dollar amount of discretionary budget authority;
  "(2) any item of new direct spending; or
  "(3) any limited tax benefit;
if the President—
  "(A) determines that such cancellation will—
    "(i) reduce the Federal budget deficit;
    "(ii) not impair any essential Government functions; and
    "(iii) not harm the national interest; and
  "(B) notifies the Congress of such cancellation by transmitting a special message, in accordance with section 1022, within five calendar days (excluding Sundays) after the enactment of the law providing the dollar amount of discretionary budget authority, item of new direct spending, or limited tax benefit that was canceled.
  "(b) IDENTIFICATION OF CANCELLATIONS.—In identifying dollar amounts of discretionary budget authority, items of new direct spending, and limited tax benefits for cancellation, the President shall—
    "(1) consider the legislative history, construction, and purposes of the law which contains such dollar amounts, items, or benefits;

Document of the U.S. House of Representatives.

"(2) consider any specific sources of information referenced in such law or, in the absence of specific sources of information, the best available information; and

"(3) use the definitions contained in section 1026 in applying this part to the specific provisions of such law.

"(c) EXCEPTION FOR DISAPPROVAL BILLS.—The authority granted by subsection (a) shall not apply to any dollar amount of discretionary budget authority, item of new direct spending, or limited tax benefit contained in any law that is a disapproval bill as defined in section 1026.

"SPECIAL MESSAGES

"SEC. 1022. (a) IN GENERAL.—For each law from which a cancellation has been made under this part, the President shall transmit a single special message to the Congress.

Congress.
2 USC 691a.

"(b) CONTENTS.—

"(1) The special message shall specify—

"(A) the dollar amount of discretionary budget authority, item of new direct spending, or limited tax benefit which has been canceled, and provide a corresponding reference number for each cancellation;

"(B) the determinations required under section 1021(a), together with any supporting material;

"(C) the reasons for the cancellation;

"(D) to the maximum extent practicable, the estimated fiscal, economic, and budgetary effect of the cancellation;

"(E) all facts, circumstances and considerations relating to or bearing upon the cancellation, and to the maximum extent practicable, the estimated effect of the cancellation upon the objects, purposes and programs for which the canceled authority was provided; and

"(F) include the adjustments that will be made pursuant to section 1024 to the discretionary spending limits under section 601 and an evaluation of the effects of those adjustments upon the sequestration procedures of section 251 of the Balanced Budget and Emergency Deficit Control Act of 1985.

"(2) In the case of a cancellation of any dollar amount of discretionary budget authority or item of new direct spending, the special message shall also include, if applicable—

"(A) any account, department, or establishment of the Government for which such budget authority was to have been available for obligation and the specific project or governmental functions involved;

"(B) the specific States and congressional districts, if any, affected by the cancellation; and

"(C) the total number of cancellations imposed during the current session of Congress on States and congressional districts identified in subparagraph (B).

"(c) TRANSMISSION OF SPECIAL MESSAGES TO HOUSE AND SENATE.—

"(1) The President shall transmit to the Congress each special message under this part within five calendar days (excluding Sundays) after enactment of the law to which the cancellation applies. Each special message shall be transmitted to the House of Representatives and the Senate on the same calendar day. Such special message shall be delivered to the

25 President Nixon's Letter of Resignation

President Nixon signed this letter of resignation on August 9, 1974, the day after his nationally televised resignation speech. The letter is addressed to the secretary of state at that time, Henry Kissinger. According to the National Archives record, the letter was in accordance with a law passed by Congress in 1792. The record of the National Archives also explains that "the letter became effective when Secretary of State, Henry Kissinger, initialed it upon receipt at 11:35 a.m."

THE WHITE HOUSE

WASHINGTON

August 9, 1974

Dear Mr. Secretary:

I hereby resign the Office of President of the United States.

Sincerely,

Richard Nixon

The Honorable Henry A. Kissinger
The Secretary of State
Washington, D.C. 20520

11.35 AM

HK

Courtesy of the National Archives.

26 Transcript of a Radio Address by President Clinton

Next is one of President Bill Clinton's radio addresses, in which he talks about two measures designed to improve food safety: that meat-packing plants and slaughterhouses will be required to conduct scientific safety tests and that food companies will be required to improve their sanitation procedures. The White House provides transcripts of the president's radio talks for the press and the public.

Courtesy of the White House.

THE WHITE HOUSE

Office of the Press Secretary

_____

For Immediate Release   July 6, 1996

RADIO ADDRESS
BY THE PRESIDENT
TO THE NATION

The Oval Office

10:06 A.M. EDT

THE PRESIDENT: Good morning. This holiday weekend we celebrate America's birthday and the values that hold us together as a community and a country. It's a time for family and fun, for games and fireworks and backyard barbecues.

Tonight, smoke will curl over homes on nearly every block as millions of families gather around the grill for the most American of meals: hamburgers and hotdogs and barbecued chicken.

Today I want to talk to you about the steps we're taking to make sure the food we cook in backyard barbecues is safe and wholesome. Our families have every right to expect the food they serve their children is safe. They have every right to expect the world's most bountiful food supply will also be the world's safest. And, in fact, our food is very safe.

Nearly a century ago, after muckrakers exposed dirty conditions in meat-packing plants, we made a national commitment to protect the public from unsafe food. It was one of the first ways we came together to meet the challenges of that new industrial age.

Last year, we put in place new safety precautions for seafood. And in recent years, we've learned that we all must continue to be vigilant on meat and poultry safety, and we learned it the hard way. For, every year, scores of Americans still die and tens of thousands become sick from eating meat or poultry that is contaminated with harmful bacteria.

We all remember how, in 1993, tragedy struck hundreds of families in the western United States. Undercooked hamburgers served in a fast food restaurant were contaminated with a deadly strain of E. coli bacterial. Five hundred people became ill and four children died.

The parents of many of the E. coli victims turned their grief into a determination to help others. Some of them are here with me today. In the face of this unspeakable tragedy, they had one insistent question: How could this have happened? I asked that question too, and I asked my administration: What can we do to prevent it from happening again?

Now, sometimes food makes us sick because it's undercooked. But sometimes, families have been exposed to illnesses because some meat and poultry shipped to our supermarket shelves contained invisible and deadly bacteria. The reason was shocking and simple: For all our technological advances, the way we inspect meat and poultry had not changed in 90 years. Even though we know that killers such as salmonella can only be seen with a microscope, inspectors were still checking on meat and poultry by look, touch, smell. We relied on an overworked cadre of government inspectors, rather than working with the industry and challenging it to keep food safe.

-more-

90

Under the direction of Vice President Gore and Secretary Glickman, the United States Department of Agriculture has worked with industry, scientists, farmers, parents and consumers to completely revamp our meat and poultry inspection system, to revolutionize the way our nation protects food safety.

This morning, I want to announce the major changes that the U.S. Department of Agriculture will take to keep food safe and to protect our children from deadly bacteria.

First, we're challenging every meat-packing plant in America to do scientific tests or take other safety precautions at every step of production. Each company must design and put in place its own tough plan. We're not imposing a detailed list of dos and don'ts. We're working with industry as partners, challenging them to find ways to make our meat the safest it can be. Each plant will be held accountable for meeting high standards at every step of the process.

Second, we're insisting that every slaughterhouse begin to conduct rigorous scientific tests to make sure the meat is not contaminated with deadly strains of E. coli and salmonella bacteria.

Third, companies will have to improve their sanitation procedures. All too often, food is contaminated because simple sanitary rules are not followed.

All these changes will be phased in over the coming months to make sure they are done right. These new meat and poultry contamination safeguards will be the strongest ever. They are flexible and they do challenge the private sector to take responsibility. They also use the most up-to-date science to track down invisible threats. They protect the public without tangling business in red tape.

Parents should know that when they serve a chicken dinner they're not putting their children at risk. Parents should know that when a teenager borrows the car to get a fast food hamburger, the hamburger should be the least of their worries. Our new food safety initiative will give families the security to know that the food they eat is as safe as it can be.

To be sure, parents will also still have to take responsibility. There is no way to make food entirely free from risk; nature simply won't let us. So everyone should follow warning labels, be careful how you handle raw meat and poultry, and make sure it's well cooked before you serve it to your family. These days families have enough to worry about. They shouldn't have to fear the food they eat is unsafe. With the tough steps we're taking today, America's parents should be able to breathe a little easier.

Have a safe and happy Fourth of July weekend.

END   10:11 A.M. EDT

One of the functions of the presidency is to be the nation's first family, fulfilling all the social roles of a regular family—keeping a home, entertaining, practicing religion, and so forth—but on a national scale, in the public eye. This holiday greeting card from the Clintons is just one example of how the first family function is performed.

We wish you the Peace of this Holiday Season and a Joyous New Year!

Bill Clinton   Hillary Rodham Clinton

Courtesy of Ms. Jerry Nestingen.

28   The Layers of Federal Bureaucracy

The organization chart of the Department of Transportation (Chart 1) reveals the breadth and depth of the U.S. federal bureaucracy. If you look at Chart 2, you will see that the Department of Transportation is only one of many departments on the organization chart of the federal executive branch. Furthermore, even one of the lowest level boxes on Chart 1— the Federal Highway Administration — has to be illustrated by another elaborate organization chart (Chart 3). The organization charts of the Department of Transportation and the executive branch are from the *1996 U.S. Government Manual,* published by the U.S. Government Printing Office. The organization chart of the Federal Highway Administration is from *The American on the Move*, a publication of the Federal Highway Administration.

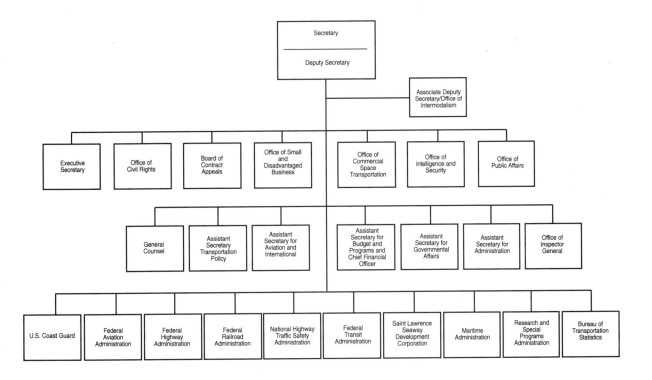

Chart 1   Department of Transportation

Courtesy of the Federal Highway Administration, the U.S. Department of Transportation, and the U.S. Government Printing Office.

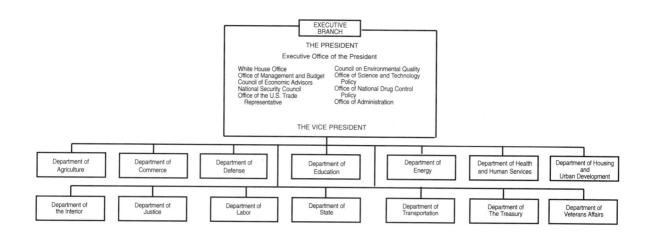

Chart 2   Executive Branch

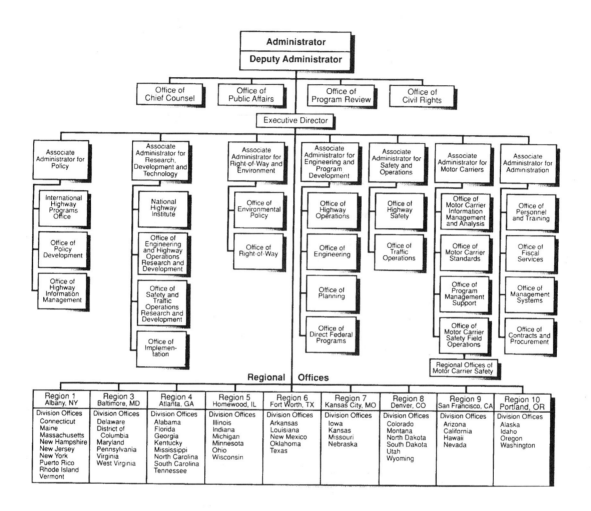

Administrator

Deputy Administrator

| Office of Chief Counsel | Office of Public Affairs | Office of Program Review | Office of Civil Rights |

Executive Director

| Associate Administrator for Policy | Associate Administrator for Research, Development and Technology | Associate Administrator for Right-of-Way and Environment | Associate Administrator for Engineering and Program Development | Associate Administrator for Safety and Operations | Associate Administrator for Motor Carriers | Associate Administrator for Administration |

| International Highway Programs Office | National Highway Institute | Office of Environmental Policy | Office of Highway Operations | Office of Highway Safety | Office of Motor Carrier Information Management and Analysis | Office of Personnel and Training |

| Office of Policy Development | Office of Engineering and Highway Operations Research and Development | Office of Right-of-Way | Office of Engineering | Office of Traffic Operations | Office of Motor Carrier Standards | Office of Fiscal Services |

| Office of Highway Information Management | Office of Safety and Traffic Operations Research and Development | | Office of Planning | | Office of Program Management Support | Office of Management Systems |

| | Office of Implementation | | Office of Direct Federal Programs | | Office of Motor Carrier Safety Field Operations | Office of Contracts and Procurement |

| | | | | | Regional Offices of Motor Carrier Safety | |

Regional Offices

Region 1 Albany, NY	Region 3 Baltimore, MD	Region 4 Atlanta, GA	Region 5 Homewood, IL	Region 6 Fort Worth, TX	Region 7 Kansas City, MO	Region 8 Denver, CO	Region 9 San Francisco, CA	Region 10 Portland, OR
Division Offices	Division Offices	Division Offices	Division Offices	Division Offices	Division Offices	Division Offices	Division Offices	Division Offices
Connecticut Maine Massachusetts New Hampshire New Jersey New York Puerto Rico Rhode Island Vermont	Delaware District of Columbia Maryland Pennsylvania Virginia West Virginia	Alabama Florida Georgia Kentucky Mississippi North Carolina South Carolina Tennessee	Illinois Indiana Michigan Minnesota Ohio Wisconsin	Arkansas Louisiana New Mexico Oklahoma Texas	Iowa Kansas Missouri Nebraska	Colorado Montana North Dakota South Dakota Utah Wyoming	Arizona California Hawaii Nevada	Alaska Idaho Oregon Washington

Chart 3   Federal Highway Administration

95

The federal bureaucracy performs a variety of functions, many too complicated, or too specific, to be understood by the general public. Nevertheless, some government agencies affect each individual's daily life. Among them is the Food Safety and Inspection Service (FSIS) of the Department of Agriculture. As a public health agency, the FSIS regulates 250,000 processed meat and poultry products as well as raw beef, pork, lamb, chicken, and turkey. In addition, the FSIS distributes a variety of publications to educate the public about food safety. Here is an excerpt from one of its publications.

Courtesy of the Food Safety and Inspection Service.

This booklet tells you what to do at each step in food handling—from shopping through storing leftovers—to avoid food poisoning.

Never had food poisoning? Actually, it's called foodborne illness. Perhaps you have, but thought you were sick with the flu. Some 33 million Americans could suffer from foodborne illness this year.

Why? Because under the right conditions, bacteria you can't see, smell or taste can make you sick.

It doesn't have to happen, though. Many such cases could be avoided if people just handled food properly. So here's what to do...

WHEN **Y**OU **S**HOP
Buy cold food last, get it home fast

- When you're out, grocery shop last. Take food straight home to the refrigerator. *Never leave food in a hot car!*

- Don't buy anything you won't use before the use-by date.

- *Don't buy food in poor condition.* Make sure refrigerated food is cold to the touch. Frozen food should be rock-solid. Canned goods should be free of dents, cracks or bulging lids which can indicate a *serious* food poisoning threat.

WHEN **Y**OU **S**TORE **F**OOD
Keep it safe, refrigerate

Check the temperature of your refrigerator with an appliance thermometer. To keep bacteria in check, the refrigerator should run at 40° F; the freezer unit at 0° F. Keep your refrigerator as cold as possible without freezing milk or lettuce.

- Freeze fresh meat, poultry or fish immediately if you can't use it within a few days.

- Put packages of raw meat, poultry or fish on a plate before refrigerating so their juices won't drip on other food. Raw juices often contain bacteria.

30 A Search Warrant

In many countries, a search warrant is issued by the public prosecutor's office, but in the United States a search warrant is issued by the courts. Hence, the U.S. court system has a reserved check on the executive branch in potential legal cases. Presented here is a search warrant that was issued by the D.C. Superior Court in a real case. The name of the accused and all personal data have been removed to protect the recipient.

Courtesy of the Superior Court of the District of Columbia.

Affidavit in Support of an Application for
Search Warrant

☐ United States
District Court

☒ Superior Court of the District
of Columbia

FOR THE ENTIRE PREMISES OF   STREET, SOUTHEAST,WASHINGTON D.C.
DESCRIBED AS A TWO STORY ATTACHED HOUSE WITH BEIGE ALUMINUM SIDING
BLACK SHUTTERS, WITH THE NUMBER   ABOVE THE MAIL BO...

Within the past seventy-two hours undercover officer Stephenson, of
the fifth district vice unit, reports that he walked to   Street
Southeast, Washington, D.C. where he approached a black male standing
outside the premises, the undercover officer asked the black male did
he have anything, the black male asked the undercover officer what did
he want, the undercover replied by saying a "twenty" the black male went
inside the premises of   Street, Southeast, Washington, D.C. and
returned within seconds with a large plastic bag which contained several
ziplocks bags with white rocks substance, the black male gave the undercover officer one ziplock bag which contained a white rock substance, the
undercover officer gave the black male one twenty dollar bill of advanced
MPDC funds, the undercover officer left and returned to his vehicle where
a field test was performed on portion of the white rock substance which
showed a postive reaction for cocaine.

The information was turned over to Inv. Burrell who had received information
that drugs was being sold and stored within the premises of   Street,
Southeast, Washington, D.C.

Based on the information that the affiant had, and the purchase of a
quanity of "Crack" Cocaine" from within the premises by undercover officer
Stephenson, the affiant believe that probable cause has been established,
and drugs are being sold and stored within the premises   Street,
Southeast, Washington, D.C. the affiant respectfully request that a Search
Warrant be issued,directing a search of the premises for narcotic drugs
and proceeds derived from the same, which is a violation of D.C. Code 33
Section 541. *Experience has taught the affiant that individuals Who sell drugs from a*
House often store drug proceeds, paraphernalia and documents and records related to the sale of
narcotics and ownership of the items, and such items should also be seized.

_____   _____ 4/1/94
        Affiant   United States Attorney

                SD
              _____
               Element

Subscribed and sworn to before me this 1st **day of** April, 19 94.

_____   _____
        Magistrate   Judge
   United States District Court   Superior Court of the District of Columbia

31 A Writ of Habeas Corpus

The right of an individual to a writ of habeas corpus is provided in Article I, Section 9, of the Constitution, even though most constitutional protections of personal liberty are in various amendments. Designed as a protection against unlawful imprisonment, the privilege of the writ is vital to due process of law. American courts issue a variety of writs of habeas corpus. Presented here is one of the three kinds issued by the Superior Court of the District of Columbia: a writ of habeas corpus ad prosequendum.

```
                                                         JUN 28 1996
        SUPERIOR COURT OF THE DISTRICT OF COLUMBIA
           CRIMINAL DIVISION - FELONY BRANCH          JUL 2  11 16 AM '96

  UNITED STATES OF AMERICA      :  CRIMINAL NO. F-10565-95

            v.                  :  JUDGE: R. DIAZ      SP1459-96

                                :  TRIAL DATE: JULY 26 1996
                                   DOB: 04/10/67

             WRIT OF HABEAS CORPUS AD PROSEQUENDUM
  THE PRESIDENT OF THE UNITED STATES:
  TO THE WARDEN FOR THE ANNE ARUNDEL COUNTY DETENTION, ANNAPOLIS,
  MARYLAND;  TO THE UNITED STATES MARSHAL FOR THE DISTRICT OF
  COLUMBIA;  SUPERIOR COURT;  TO THE UNITED STATES MARSHAL FOR THE
  STATE OF MARYLAND:
  GREETINGS:
        You are hereby commanded to produce the body of _____
  __ __ __ by you imprisoned and detained as it is said, to either the
  United States Marshal in and for the District of Columbia or the
  United States Marshal for the STATE OF MARYLAND, and under safe and
  secure conduct, before the Superior Court of the District of
  Columbia on JULY 23, 1996 at 9:00 a.m., so that ____ _____ ___
  may be present for TRIAL DATE on JULY 26, 1996 in the above-
  captioned case in this Court and, then, upon the conclusion of such
  proceedings be returned to the jurisdiction from whence he came and
  have then and there this writ.
                                           JUDGE
                                   BY
                                           DEPUTY CLERK

  Executed this writ in the
  above-entitled case, the
  ___ day of _____ 1996.     UNITED STATES MARSHAL    A TRUE COPY
                                                        TEST: 7-2-96
  BY: _____          _____
           Deputy Marshal       DATE
                                              Clerk, Superior Court of the
                                              District of Columbia
                                              By _____
```

Courtesy of the Superior Court of the District of Columbia.

Each judge has his or her own style of giving instructions to a jury. Here are some of the instructions that were given to the jury by Judge Colleen Kollar-Kotelly, the Deputy Presiding Judge of the Criminal Division of the D.C. Superior Court, in a trial in early 1996. The person on trial was accused of six offenses; the excerpt is the judge's instructions regarding the second offense, armed robbery.

ARMED ROBBERY

The defendant has been charged as acting as a principal and/or an aider and abettor for this charge.

The defendant is charged with Armed Robbery. I am going to instruct you on this charge and also on the lesser included offenses of Robbery and Theft. After I give you the elements of these crimes, I will tell you in what order you should consider them.

I. ARMED ROBBERY

The essential elements of the offense of armed robbery, each of which the government must prove beyond a reasonable doubt, are:

1.   That the defendant took property of some value from the complainant, against the complainant's will;

2.   That the defendant took the property belonging to "Up Against the Wall" from the immediate actual possession of the complainant, Kerwin Wilson, or from his person;

3.   That the defendant used force or violence to take the property, by using actual physical force or violence and/or putting the complainant in fear;

4.   That the defendant carried the property away;

5.   That the defendant took the property without right to it, and with the specific intent to steal it; and

6.   That at the time of the offense, the defendant was armed as follows: (a) the defendant, acting as an aider and abettor, was

---

Courtesy of the Superior Court of the District of Columbia.

armed with a sawed off rifle; and/or (b) the defendant, acting as a principal, was armed with a pellet gun.

To take property means to get possession of it, so as to be able to exercise control over it. The taking must be against the will of the complainant, because no robbery occurs if the complainant knows about and consents to the taking, or some other authorized person consents on the owner's behalf. The property must have had some value, but the amount of value is not important and the government does not have to prove it had a particular money value.

Property is in the immediate actual possession of the complainant if it is located on the complainant's person or close enough that one could reasonably expect the complainant to exercise physical control over it.

To establish a robbery, it is not sufficient that the defendant simply took the property; he must have taken it by using force or violence.

Using actual force or physical violence against the complainant so as to overcome or prevent the complainant's resistance satisfies the requirement of force or violence.

Putting the complainant in fear, without using actual force or physical violence, can satisfy the requirement of force or violence if the circumstances, such as threats by words or gestures, would in common experience, create a reasonable fear of danger and cause a person to give up the clothing in order to avoid physical harm.

It is necessary that the defendant carried away the property after taking it, so as to deprive the complainant of its possession, but the least removal of the thing from its place can be enough to show carrying away.

The government must establish that the defendant had no right to take the property, and that he had the specific intent to steal it. There can be no robbery if the defendant takes the property for a lawful purpose. It is necessary that the defendant had the specific intent to deprive the complainant of the complainant's property and to convert it and keep it for the defendant's own use and benefit.

33 A Supreme Court Decision, *Bush v. Vera*

On July 13, 1996, a 5–4 Supreme Court vote nullified three Texas congressional districts located in Dallas and Houston; these districts had been redrawn on the basis of the 1990 census. In the opinion of the Court (*Bush v. Vera*), the three congressional districts were unconstitutional because state legislators had overemphasized race in redrawing the districts.

There was no majority opinion in the decision on *Bush v. Vera*. Justice Sandra Day O'Connor wrote a plurality opinion in which she made a detailed, case-by-case analysis of the three districts. Her plurality opinion was joined by Chief Justice William H. Rehnquist and Justice Anthony M. Kennedy. Not satisfied that she had fully expressed her own ideas on the issue, Justice O'Connor then added an opinion signed only by her. Justices Clarence Thomas and Antonin Scalia, who agreed that the Texas districts were unconstitutional, refused to sign either of Justice O'Connor's opinions. Instead, Justice Thomas wrote a concurring opinion that Justice Scalia also signed. Justices John Paul Stevens and David H. Souter each wrote dissenting opinions, which were also signed by Justices Ruth Bader Ginsburg and Stephen G. Breyer. The first page of each opinion is included here. The entire document is over one hundred pages long.

Supreme Court document.

(Slip Opinion)

SUPREME COURT OF THE UNITED STATES

Syllabus

BUSH, GOVERNOR OF TEXAS, ET AL. *v.* VERA ET AL.

APPEAL FROM THE DISTRICT COURT FOR THE SOUTHERN DISTRICT OF TEXAS

No. 94–805. Argued December 5, 1995—Decided June 13, 1996*

Because the 1990 census revealed a population increase entitling Texas to three additional congressional seats, and in an attempt to comply with the Voting Rights Act of 1965 (VRA), the Texas Legislature promulgated a redistricting plan that, among other things, created District 30 as a new majority-African-American district in Dallas County and District 29 as a new majority-Hispanic district in Harris County, and reconfigured District 18, which is adjacent to District 29, as a majority-African-American district. After the Department of Justice precleared the plan under VRA §5, the plaintiffs, six Texas voters, filed this challenge alleging that 24 of the State's 30 congressional districts constitute racial gerrymanders in violation of the Fourteenth Amendment. The three-judge District Court held Districts 18, 29, and 30 unconstitutional. The Governor of Texas, private intervenors, and the United States (as intervenor) appeal.

Held: The judgment is affirmed.

861 F. Supp. 1304, affirmed.

JUSTICE O'CONNOR, joined by THE CHIEF JUSTICE and JUSTICE KENNEDY, concluded:

1. Plaintiff Chen, who resides in District 25 and has not alleged any specific facts showing that he personally has been subjected to

---

* Together with No. 94–806, *Lawson et al.* v. *Vera et al.,* and No. 94–988, *United States* v. *Vera et al.,* also on appeal from the same court.

I

Syllabus

but for its affirmative use of racial demographics. Assuming that the State has asserted a compelling state interest, its redistricting attempts were not narrowly tailored to achieve that interest. Pp. 1–5.

O'CONNOR, J., announced the judgment of the Court and delivered an opinion, in which REHNQUIST, C. J., and KENNEDY, J., joined. O'CONNOR, J., also filed a separate concurring opinion. KENNEDY, J., filed a concurring opinion. THOMAS, J., filed an opinion concurring in the judgment, in which SCALIA, J., joined. STEVENS, J., filed a dissenting opinion, in which GINSBURG and BREYER, JJ., joined. SOUTER, J., filed a dissenting opinion, in which GINSBURG and BREYER, JJ., joined.

SUPREME COURT OF THE UNITED STATES

Nos. 94–805, 94–806 AND 94–988

GEORGE W. BUSH, GOVERNOR OF TEXAS, ET AL., APPELLANTS

94–805   *v.*

AL VERA ET AL.

WILLIAM LAWSON, ET AL., APPELLANTS

94–806   *v.*

AL VERA ET AL.

UNITED STATES, APPELLANT

94–988   *v.*

AL VERA ET AL.

ON APPEALS FROM THE UNITED STATES DISTRICT COURT FOR THE SOUTHERN DISTRICT OF TEXAS

[June 13, 1996]

JUSTICE O'CONNOR announced the judgment of the Court and delivered an opinion, in which THE CHIEF JUSTICE and JUSTICE KENNEDY join.

This is the latest in a series of appeals involving racial gerrymandering challenges to state redistricting efforts in the wake of the 1990 census. See *Shaw* v. *Hunt, ante,* p. ___ *(Shaw II); United States* v. *Hays,* 515 U. S. ___ (1995); *Miller* v. *Johnson,* 515 U. S. ___ (1995); *Shaw* v. *Reno,* 509 U. S. 630 (1993) *(Shaw I).* That census revealed a population increase, largely in urban minority populations, that entitled Texas to three additional congressional seats. In response, and with a view to complying with the Voting Rights Act of 1965 (VRA), 79 Stat. 437, as amended, 42 U. S. C. §1973 *et seq.,* the Texas Legislature promulgated a redistricting

SUPREME COURT OF THE UNITED STATES

Nos. 94–805, 94–806 AND 94–988

GEORGE W. BUSH, GOVERNOR OF TEXAS, ET AL.,
APPELLANTS
94–805   *v.*
AL VERA ET AL.

WILLIAM LAWSON, ET AL., APPELLANTS
94–806   *v.*
AL VERA ET AL.

UNITED STATES, APPELLANT
94–988   *v.*
AL VERA ET AL.

ON APPEALS FROM THE UNITED STATES DISTRICT COURT
FOR THE SOUTHERN DISTRICT OF TEXAS

[June 13, 1996]

JUSTICE O'CONNOR, concurring.

I write separately to express my view on two points. First, compliance with the results test of §2 of the Voting Rights Act (VRA) is a compelling state interest. Second, that test can co-exist in principle and in practice with *Shaw* v. *Reno*, 509 U. S. 630 (1993), and its progeny, as elaborated in today's opinions.

I

As stated in the plurality opinion, *ante*, at 23 (O'CONNOR, J., joined by REHNQUIST, C. J., and KENNEDY J.), this Court has thus far assumed without deciding that compliance with the results test of VRA §2(b) is a compelling state interest. See *Shaw* v. *Hunt*, ___ U. S. ___, ___ (1996) *(Shaw II)* [draft op. at 13]; *Miller* v.

SUPREME COURT OF THE UNITED STATES

Nos. 94–805, 94–806 AND 94–988

GEORGE W. BUSH, GOVERNOR OF TEXAS, ET AL.,
APPELLANTS
94–805   *v.*
AL VERA ET AL.

WILLIAM LAWSON, ET AL., APPELLANTS
94–806   *v.*
AL VERA ET AL.

UNITED STATES, APPELLANT
94–988   *v.*
AL VERA ET AL.

ON APPEALS FROM THE UNITED STATES DISTRICT COURT
FOR THE SOUTHERN DISTRICT OF TEXAS

[June 13, 1996]

JUSTICE KENNEDY, concurring.

I join the plurality opinion, but the statements in Part II of the opinion that strict scrutiny would not apply to all cases of intentional creation of majority-minority districts, *ante,* at 3, 7–8, require comment. Those statements are unnecessary to our decision, for strict scrutiny applies here. I do not consider these dicta to commit me to any position on the question whether race is predominant whenever a State, in redistricting, foreordains that one race be the majority in a certain number of districts or in a certain part of the State. In my view, we would no doubt apply strict scrutiny if a State decreed that certain districts had to be at least 50 percent white, and our analysis should be no different if the State so favors minority races.

SUPREME COURT OF THE UNITED STATES

Nos. 94–805, 94–806 AND 94–988

GEORGE W. BUSH, GOVERNOR OF TEXAS, ET AL.,
APPELLANTS
94–805   *v.*
AL VERA ET AL.

WILLIAM LAWSON, ET AL., APPELLANTS
94–806   *v.*
AL VERA ET AL.

UNITED STATES, APPELLANT
94–988   *v.*
AL VERA ET AL.

ON APPEALS FROM THE UNITED STATES DISTRICT COURT
FOR THE SOUTHERN DISTRICT OF TEXAS

[June 13, 1996]

JUSTICE THOMAS, with whom JUSTICE SCALIA joins,
concurring in the judgment.

In my view, application of strict scrutiny in this case
was never a close question. I cannot agree with JUSTICE
O'CONNOR's assertion that strict scrutiny is not invoked
by the intentional creation of majority-minority districts.
See *ante*, at 3. Though *Shaw* v. *Reno*, 509 U. S. 630,
649 (1993) *(Shaw I)*, expressly reserved that question,
we effectively resolved it in subsequent cases. Only last
Term, in *Adarand Constructors, Inc.* v. *Pena*, 515 U. S.
__, __ (1995) (slip op., at 25–26), we vigorously asserted
that all governmental racial classifications must be

SUPREME COURT OF THE UNITED STATES

Nos. 94–805, 94–806 AND 94–988

GEORGE W. BUSH, GOVERNOR OF TEXAS, ET AL.,
APPELLANTS
94–805   *v.*
AL VERA ET AL.

WILLIAM LAWSON, ET AL., APPELLANTS
94–806   *v.*
AL VERA ET AL.

UNITED STATES, APPELLANT
94–988   *v.*
AL VERA ET AL.

ON APPEALS FROM THE UNITED STATES DISTRICT COURT
FOR THE SOUTHERN DISTRICT OF TEXAS

[June 13, 1996]

JUSTICE STEVENS, with whom JUSTICE GINSBURG and
JUSTICE BREYER join, dissenting.

The 1990 census revealed that Texas' population had
grown, over the past decade, almost twice as fast as the
population of the country as a whole. As a result, Texas
was entitled to elect three additional Representatives to
the United States Congress, enlarging its delegation
from 27 to 30. Because Texas' growth was concentrated
in South Texas and the cities of Dallas and Houston, the
state legislature concluded that the new congressional
districts should be carved out of existing districts in
those areas. The consequences of the political battle
that produced the new map are some of the most oddly
shaped congressional districts in the United States.

Today, the Court strikes down three of Texas' majority-

SUPREME COURT OF THE UNITED STATES

———

Nos. 94–805, 94–806 AND 94–988

———

GEORGE W. BUSH, GOVERNOR OF TEXAS, ET AL.,
APPELLANTS
94–805   *v.*
AL VERA ET AL.

WILLIAM LAWSON, ET AL., APPELLANTS
94–806   *v.*
AL VERA ET AL.

UNITED STATES, APPELLANT
94–988   *v.*
AL VERA ET AL.

ON APPEALS FROM THE UNITED STATES DISTRICT COURT
FOR THE SOUTHERN DISTRICT OF TEXAS

[June 13, 1996]

JUSTICE SOUTER, with whom JUSTICE GINSBURG and JUSTICE BREYER join, dissenting.

When the Court devises a new cause of action to enforce a constitutional provision, it ought to identify an injury distinguishable from the consequences of concededly constitutional conduct, and it should describe the elements necessary and sufficient to make out such a claim. Nothing less can give notice to those whose conduct may give rise to liability or provide standards for courts charged with enforcing the Constitution. Those principles of justification, fair notice, and guidance, have never been satisfied in the instance of the action announced three Terms ago in *Shaw* v. *Reno*, 509 U. S. 630 (1993) (*Shaw I*), when a majority of this Court decided that a State violates the Fourteenth